THE TWISTY TRAIL FROM HOMER TO COPERNICUS: A BIRD'S EYE VIEW

Dan Madden

The Twisty Trail

Copyright, 2018 by Daniel Madden

Printed by CreateSpace, an Amazon.com Company

ISBN 13: 978-1696267311

TABLE OF CONTENTS

ABOUT THE BOOK: 5
ABOUT THE AUTHOR: 7
ACKNOWLEDGMENTS: 9
PREFACE: 11
Chapter 1: MEDITERRANEAN WORLD BEFORE 1000 BCE 13
Chapter 2: THE IRON AGE IN THE EAST, 1000-500. 23
Chapter 3: The IRON AGE IN THE WEST, 1000 to 500 BCE. 29
Chapter 4: THE AGE OF PERSIAN HEGEMONY, 500 to 338 BCE. 35
Chapter 5: GREECE AND MACEDONIA, 500 to 338 BCE 41
Chapter 6: HELLENISTIC ERA IN THE EAST, 338 to 146 BCE. 51
Chapter 7: HELLENISTIC INFLUENCE IN THE WEST, 338 to 146 BCE. 57
Chapter 8: BIRTH PANGS OF THE EMPIRE, 146 BCE to 60 BCE. 65
Chapter 9: BIRTH OF THE EMPIRE, 60 BCE to 18 CE. 73
Chapter 10: GOLDEN AGE OF ROMAN CULTURE, 60 BCE to 18 CE. 79
Chapter 11: CULTURAL TRANSITION, 100-600 CE. 87
Chapter 12: THE ISLAMIC YEARS, 600-1031 CE. 99
Chapter 13: THE AGE OF REDISCOVERY, 1000-1400 CE 109
Chapter 14: BLOSSOMING BEGINS, 1400-1550 121
Chapter 15: A BIRD'S EYE VIEW: 133
LIST OF MAPS: 137
LIST OF IMAGES: 139
SELECT BIBLIOGRAPHY: 143
ENDNOTES: 147

APPENDIX: 155

INDEX: 163

ABOUT THE BOOK:

The Twisty Trail tells the turbulent tale of our Classical legacy. Amid a world of bloody warfare, looting, and destruction of cities, Ancient Greece produced a fabulous trove of literary, scientific and philosophical literature that conquering Macedonians and Romans chose to preserve and enhance. But, then, the Great Wheel of Fortune turned. After the Fall of Rome, **Twisty** tells how it was nearly lost and then was found.

The Twisty Trail

ABOUT THE AUTHOR:

Dan Madden has loved history since his high school days at John's Prep School in Danvers, MA. He obtained a BA at Boston College, Chestnut Hill, MA, in 1966 with a specialty in European History. Next, he earned his MA and Ph.D. at the University of Wisconsin- Madison in 1968 and 1972, respectively.

Dan continued to read obsessively in both American and Ancient history. Go Figure!

He began writing this book to organize his thoughts on several of his recent readings on Ancient History as they relate to the United States.

He lives in Englewood, Florida, with his wonderful wife and amazing pet lovebird, Sunshine! He and Judy have two children who live in Wisconsin and Arizona. Also, they have two fabulous grandsons.

The Twisty Trail

ACKNOWLEDGMENTS:

I am so grateful for all those who encouraged me write and publish this book. My fellow members of the Englewood Authors Club of Florida, and especially our club leader Ed Ellis, are experienced and encouraging. Also, the patient and skilled staff at Englewood's Elsie Quirk library helped me grasp the technical issues involved in using Amazon Create Space.

I am also blessed with close friends and family capable of lending a skilled hand. Judy Madden, Rick Sline and Anna Boulton read early drafts and got me on the right track. Ryan Madden, Al Rulis, and Richard Werking read the whole manuscript and provided wise commentary.

My largest debt is to Kathleen Konicek-Moran for designing such a superb and creative book cover. I figure many folks will buy the book just to get the cover.

Each of those above helped me toward my goal of producing an easy, informative overview of these centuries for casual readers, and I am very, very, grateful to each of them.

If this book accomplishes that for you, the reader, the credit goes to them. If not, I hope the book inspires and encourages you to read further on this topic anyway. Books in the Select Bibliography are a good place to start

The Twisty Trail

PREFACE:

At some point in our lives, many of us come to wonder where we came from, our genealogy. Similarly, descendants of Europeans might notice they have some unique notions about the ideal form of government and some cultural preferences distinct from that of people in many other places. Where did these come from?

A good place to begin is with Greece, around 750 or so BCE (*aka* Before the Christian Era or BC). There, someone figured out that if he added some vowels to the Phoenician alphabet, she could write down the poetic lyrics of Homer's <u>Iliad</u> and <u>Odyssey</u> and others in a manner that mimics the sound and cadence they loved to hear.

There is a big story here! The "Greek Miracle" was an astounding aberration from its past and from its own times. From 509 to 338 BCE, there was an amazing burst of thought about, and practice of, more democratic values. Simultaneously, there was an unprecedented outburst of culture. By "culture", I mean ideas and tools that societies can build on to improve the quality of individual lives: traditionally these include both arts (sculpture, architecture, theater, literature, histories, rhetoric) and scientific thinking (philosophy, astronomy, medicine, mathematics). The Greeks of this period were the first to leave a cultural trail on all these topics that has survived.

While early Greeks laid the foundation and framework for our ancient cultural homestead, succeeding generations of

Macedonians, Romans, Early Christians and Muslims will add new wiring, plumbing, and especially windows. Lady Luck plays a big role, and there are some "near death" experiences. There is also a "rebirth and rediscovery" of Greco-Roman culture in Italy and elsewhere in the 1300s, in a movement, later called "the Renaissance".

Part of what makes the story so dramatic is that Greece was such an unlikely candidate for a cultural breakthrough! Egypt and Mesopotamia were much wealthier. They had sophisticated bureaucracies and more advanced architecture and some significant beginnings in writing and art. Phoenicians had developed the first alphabet and papyrus; Israel had its Bible. By contrast, before 800 BCE Greece had a Dark Age and we know pretty little about its achievements before that!

So this tour of our ancient world begins with a quick survey of the neighborhood's history and focuses throughout on the key events from our cultural past: less about battles and empires, more about Ancient contributions to the growing of our Western Culture.

This story needs re-telling! Europe and America have been building on the Renaissance since it started! For Americans and the American Revolution, in particular, there is a strong debt to the Ancient Greeks. They were among the few to seriously consider, **and practice**, other options to governing than hereditary kingship! Europe and the Americas have been experimenting with such options ever since!

Chapter 1: MEDITERRANEAN WORLD BEFORE 1000 BCE

So, let's begin prospecting for some golden nuggets: signs of early democratic thought or of writings that might have influenced Classic Culture.

What do I mean when I refer to " Ancient Mediterranean World"? Of course, it includes the areas that now border the Great Middle Sea from Gibraltar to Lebanon, but realistically, also the Arabian Peninsula, Iran, Sudan and Coastal Pakistan.

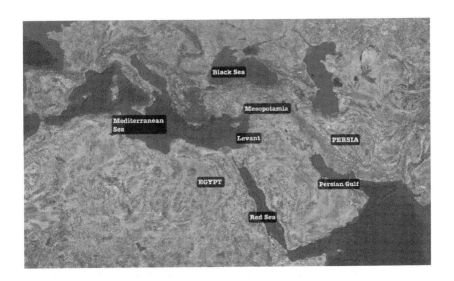

Sources: Tellers of History base their reporting on actual artifacts or writings from that time (or reasonably near). For this era (*aka* the Bronze Age), we have to imagine a world without web sites, printing, paper or even parchment.

They are limited to inscriptions carved onto buildings, rock walls or stone, or writings found on clay tablets or, less commonly, papyrus. The clay tablets display a cuneiform (made with wedge-shaped reeds) script. The scribe wrote onto wet clay tablets with a reed stylus and then baked the tablet to make it last longer. The language on the tablets used a combination of pictures and lettering to represent words and syllables. Once the modern world adopted alphabetic systems, no one living centuries later could read these earlier ones.

So, much of what we now know about Egypt came after 1834 when a French scholar published his book deciphering the Rosetta Stone Code. This enabled subsequent scholars to read Ancient Egyptian writing (a system that used word pictures, called hieroglyphics, rather than an alphabet that reflected the sounds of their spoken words).

Similarly, a British scholar, who studied the Persian King Darius's Wall Inscription (carved into the side of a cliff), published a memoir in 1849. This led he and others to decipher the three key languages of Mesopotamia. They could do this because the King's proclamation was posted on the wall in three languages. They were all cuneiform in style of script, but also pictographic. This writing method was the primary diplomatic and official communication tool throughout Mesopotamia until the Greek phonetic system gradually replaced it after 300 BCE.

So, after 1850, scholars could translate the 10,000 Hittite clay tablets found near their capital, Hattusa, in Asia Minor as well as the 30,000 clay tablets found in Nineveh (Ancient Assyria) at the site of King Ashurbanipal's Library. While wax and papyrus documents existed in Mesopotamia, few had survived due to the moist climate. Inscriptions written on the wet surface of a dry tablet and sun dried could later be erased and reused. If baked in an oven, it lasted much longer. What we have then are the baked ones.

HAND-HELD CLAY TABLET:

Ironically, then, much of this region's ancient history was only recently learned. On the other
hand, the basis for the power of both Egypt and

Mesopotamia has been understood for a long time.

The Egyptian Empire lasted for 31 dynasties that trace from 3200 to 332 BCE. Its wealth and influence were due to:
(1) Its control through irrigation of the Nile River Valley, a major producer of wheat and grain during this entire era and those to come;
(2) Geographic protection on the east and west by desert;
(3) Its pivotal location at the nexus of the Mediterranean and the Red Sea that enabled its kings to grow wealthy serving as middlemen for trade between these regions and India.

This Empire reached its peak under Thutmose I (1504-1492 BCE) when it reached north to the Euphrates River and south to the 4th Cataract--well into Nubia (Sudan).

Egyptian kings left behind a substantial physical record that includes giant pyramids, royal tombs, papyrus scrolls, clay tablets, wall art, and bureaucratic records. Egyptians were already writing with hieroglyphics (pictograms) as early as 3200 BCE. Two papyrus documents survive from 2400 BCE including one that describes how the Great Pyramid of Giza was constructed. Otherwise, much of what has survived from the Bronze Age is trade or bureaucracy related, but it all opens windows to our understanding of the period: one surviving religious and magical narrative from this era is The Book of the Dead that describes funeral procedures (1550 BCE). Few of the scrolls are historical or biographical, but one of these is the Great Harris Papyrus, (12th Century BCE), 40 meters long

(4 times the usual length) which describes the very successful reign of Ramses III. At least 10 dealt with scientific, medical or mathematical issues; another seven

MAP OF FERTILE CRESCENT, 1450 BCE:

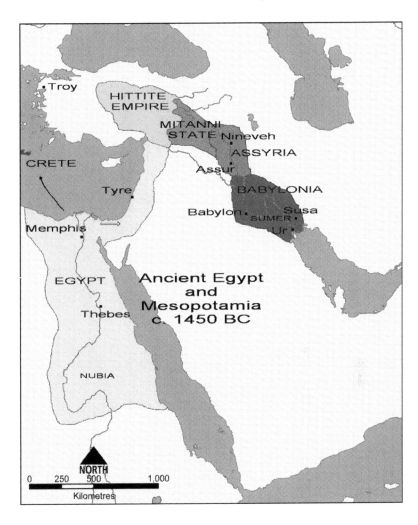

were literary in intent, including The Eloquent Peasant, 1859-40 BCE. Had westerners been able to read them, they might have impacted Western thought and culture.

Mesopotamia nurtured a civilization as ancient as Egypt. Its oldest settlements date between 4900 and 3500 BCE compared to Egypt's oldest known city in 3600. Sumerians were writing in cuneiform script on baked clay tablets by 3300. Of the 13 or so documents (tablets or papyrus) that survive from either Egypt or Sumer (who ruled Mesopotamia at the time), and originate before 2000, eight are Sumerian.

The history of this area appears more tumultuous than Egypt: Ur ruled the region from 3800 to 3200 BCE; Sumerians from 2330 to 2000; Assyrians from 1900 to 1400. There were three good reasons the area was fought over:

(1). Situated at the junction of the Tigris and Euphrates as well as the Persian Gulf, its location was pivotal.
(2). Further, major roads (the Royal Road from Persia to the Aegean) passed through or near it and these facilitated trade (but also invasions) between the Aegean Sea and Southeastern Iran.
(3). Control of this region required a well organized society simply to manage the irrigation system that enabled food production in an otherwise arid region.

Mesopotamian kings also left an impressive physical record: 22 clay tablets that date between 1600 and 2400 BCE. They produced ziggurats (a Persian Temple) rather than pyramids, but clay tablets and cuneiform writings abound. There also are quite detailed records of contracts, proclamations, and royal inscriptions on temples and tombs. Surviving narrative literary achievements include the <u>Lamentation on the Destruction of Ur</u> and the <u>Gilgamesh Epic</u>, an early creation narrative with a flood story, each between 2150 and 2004 BCE.

The documents we have, and can now read, show that these two Empires battled one another (and others) throughout with neither conquering the other. The battle and subsequent treaty of Kadesh (1275 BCE) marks the high-water point for both Egypt and the Hittites (recent conquerors of Mesopotamia), as the two great heavyweights finally agree on the Euphrates River as a boundary between them.

The documents we have also describe three other civilizations that enter the stage at the very end portion of the Bronze age:

Hittites, for a time, posed a serious threat to both of these larger Empires. Initially, they settled and dominated eastern and central Anatolia (Turkey) from 1700 to 1500 BCE. Next, over the following 200 years, they conquered Cyprus and swept through much of Northern Mesopotamia and northern Palestine. Seemingly unstoppable, they confronted Egypt and Ramses ll at the famous Battle of Kadesh in about 1275 BCE. This halted their advance and, shortly thereafter, they signed a treaty of alliance with Egypt.

Over the next 50 years or so, the Hittite Empire, under pressure from both the "Sea Peoples" and from the Assyrians, gradually dissolved. Assyrians destroyed their capital, Hattusa, in 1180. Because Hittites left behind a trove of over 10,000 clay tablets in their royal archives, we know much about their history, governance and religion, but not much about the reasons for their demise.

Phoenicia is the name Greeks gave to the coalition of independent city-states that emerged along the shores of the Levant when Egypt and the Hittites slowly evacuated the region after 1200 BCE. These cities, Byblos, Tyre, Sidon, and Anshar, were walled and well protected from land attack.

The Phoenician were a seagoing people whose economy was based on transporting goods, which was 10 time less expensive than goods transported by land. Key citizens were merchants and traders in purple dye, cedar, shellfish, wine, olive oil and papyrus. Their leading city was Byblos, one of the world's oldest, with evidence of settlements dating to 5000 BCE.

Unlike the Hittites, they left no troves of archival clay tablets. They did provide palace ruins and inscriptions; also there are important references to them in documents in the archives of the Egyptians and Babylonians. Specifically, there are letters from the Byblos leaders written to Egyptian governors asking them for military help. Dated at 1350 BCE, the language suggests Byblos had a subservient relationship with Egypt at the time. Further, royal inscriptions at Byblos, show that Phoenicians had invented the first alphabet by 1200 BCE. They used only 22 letters, all consonants.

Crete: Minoan Civilization was an island culture centered at Knossos in the 12th and 13th centuries BCE. Scholars have detected a connection between Knossos and Egypt and between Knossos and Mycenae in Greece. In the later years, they used a non-phonetic language called <u>Linear b</u> which has similarities with early Greek. The civilization was destroyed in a volcanic eruption. I have been to Knossos and was very impressed with their art and architecture. Additional archaeological finds might connect it more firmly to Classical Greece, but it all seems speculative at this point.

Reflection: I find it hard to single out any individual cultural or political achievements important to Western democracies during the Bronze Age. After all, before 1834, their documents were unintelligible to either European or Middle-eastern scholars; their government was theocratic and unlimited; their ziggurats and pyramids are stunning, but with no clear impact on Classical building techniques in the West.

Further, many of the available records of the Bronze Age (3500-1000 BCE) do mainly document battles, slaughter, and empires back and forth. While there is evidence of early writing, bureaucratic records, and sophisticated construction techniques, there is little early art or literature, even if Westerners had been able to translate it!

Even so, the end of the Bronze period sets the stage for what is to come. By 1000 BCE, both of the two powerful and wealthy civilizations of the era, Mesopotamia and Egypt, are faltering. A third, the Hittites, who also possessed substantial clay tablet records, has already risen and fallen.

As these three tides recede, a fourth, **Phoenicia** is emerging. It is different from the others in being a league of independent city-states rather than a land-based empire. Located in cities along the Eastern coast of the Mediterranean, it capitalizes on the competitive economic advantage that seafaring nations possess. They are wealthy and, by 1250 BCE, have invented the first known alphabet and used it in commerce and government.

Iconic Event: For me, the event that best represents the spirit of these centuries is the Treaty of Kadesh in 1275. First, it illustrates that these two forces, Egypt and Mesopotamia were never able to conquer one another during this whole era. It reminds me, secondly, that both Egypt and the Hittites are much weaker by the

RAMSES II VICTORY OVER HITTITES:

end of the Bronze age. Finally, though both are very literate societies, comparatively little is known about their literature or sciences.

Chapter 2: THE IRON AGE IN THE EAST, 1000-500.

My first acquaintance with the great powers of this era was through the eyes of Old Testament Israelites. The story of Jonah and the Whale involves the Assyrians of Nineveh. Daniel's Lions Den occurs during the Babylonian Captivity. The Books of Esther, Nehemiah, and Ezra describe life under Persian rule!

Looking through our chosen prisms of governmental style and cultural milestones, though, the first 500 years of the Iron Age in the East offer little different from the previous age. The method of governance remains that of absolute and hereditary kingship. Indeed, the centralization of power grows exponentially when, after 750 BCE, the Assyrians effectively move south to control the cities of Phoenicia as well as Judea.

Assyrians, conquerors of the Hittites, were the first Mediterranean "superpower" to benefit from the declines of Babylon and Egypt. Their Empire is called Neo-Assyrian to distinguish it from the earlier Assyrians that previously dominated Mesopotamia for the 500 years from 1900-1400 BCE. At that time their capital was Ashur, a city on the upper Tigris located along the Great Royal Road between Sardis in Western Anatolia (Turkey) to Susa in Persia (Iran). The new Empire's capital would also locate on the Tigris but further south at Nineveh.

Even after they destroyed Hittite power, the initial century from 1000 to 900 BCE brought balance among several powers-rather than dominance by a single nation.

Neo-Assyria, though, had a standing army, an aggressive attitude, and a fearsome and sadistic approach to captives. Their empire grew slowly from 900 to 750. But, then, from 750 to 650 BCE, three successive kings added Eastern Anatolia, Byblos (738 BCE), Israel (732), Cyprus (709),and Syria into the empire. They also conquered Egypt, sacking Memphis in 671 and Thebes in 663. This was the first Empire to control both Mesopotamia and Egypt. A very big deal!

Assyria also left behind tens of thousands of clay tablets and clay cylinders (easier to carry than tablets?); evidence of aqueducts and irrigation systems; an extensive library, where King Ashurbanipal stored the scrolls and tablets he and his ancestors looted; and early examples of zoological and botanical parks.

When the Assyrian Empire fell, though, it fell suddenly and hard. A coalition of Medes, Persians and Babylonians razed their chief cities, Ashur and Nineveh, and decisively defeated their remaining army at the Battle of Carchemish in 605.

Babylonians were the most immediate beneficiary of this battle. They assumed, and added to, the Assyrian domain by conquering Judah (586 BCE), Cyprus (546), Byblos, and retaining Egypt. They continued their own marvelous recordkeeping systems.

In 531, though, the **Persians** toppled them, and by 521, created the largest and richest Empire the region had seen! The famous Wall Inscription in Behistun, Persia, (mentioned earlier) asserts that Darius the Great's empire extends from the Indus River to Asia Minor; the Sudan to the Danube.

PERSIAN EMPIRE:

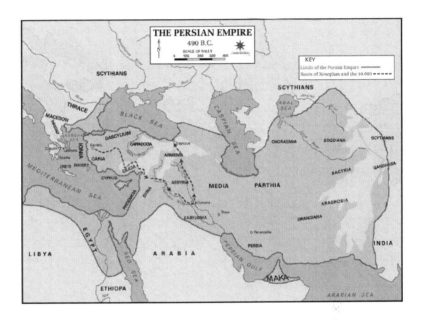

From a cultural heritage perspective, these three sophisticated, wealthy, and powerful empires of Assyria, Babylon, and Persia were all absolute kingships. Surprisingly, they left no evidence that their art or culture had a subsequent influence on the West. A significant exception is the Great Library of Ashurbanipal.

Great Library of Ashurbanipal: Archaeologists discovered this trove in the mid-nineteenth century, located in Nineveh in present day Iraq. There were over 30,000 cuneiform clay tablets, organized by subject matter. While many documents were archival, administrative or religious, several were works of literature including a 4000-year-old copy of the Epic of Gilgamesh. The library was founded sometime in the 7th century and mainly consisted of looted documents from defeated peoples.

Reflection: While these library documents themselves had no obvious impact on the culture of Western Europe, the idea itself of a great library as a place to store important literary or scientific achievements was a notion that continued on and enabled the survival of most of what we have from the Classical Era.

While my own local library, here in Englewood, Florida, avoids looting as a method of expanding its collections, it clearly played an important role in the Ancient World. (Ha, ha).

Iconic Event: Darius's Wall Inscription at Behistun (521) reminds me that the Persian Empire was the

largest ever seen to that point: it included Mesopotamia, Egypt, Libya and part of India. Equally notable, the inscription is repeated in three pre-phonetic, cuneiform languages. In short, as late as 521 BCE, the Persian Empire did not use a phonetic language. Further, some clay tablets, dated 457, and found in Persepolis are also in that same pre-phonetic cuneiform (Waters, pp. 103-108). As such, this reminds us that our understanding of Ancient Persia's cultural achievements would have to wait until after 1848 CE when phonetics-based scholars could finally decipher what they saw there.

The Twisty Trail

Chapter 3: The IRON AGE IN THE WEST, 1000 to 500 BCE.

The east Mediterranean powers, if they thought at all about the west, considered it a backwater. Indeed, one of the three key western civilizations, Carthage, only claims an independent existence after 573 BCE. A second, Rome, asserts a founding date of 753, and to have been a Republic since 509. All three statements are legends without any supporting inscriptions or writing. The third, Greece, a collection of islands, caught the attention of the Persians when these Ionians destroyed Sardis, its westernmost provincial capital, in 498.

Even so, for us prospectors panning for some golden nuggets of cultural heritage, Greece will provide an unmistakable glimmer. Let's begin though with Carthage.

Carthage in North Africa is a good example of how little evidence we have for this period in the West. Legend says it was founded and colonized by the Phoenician city, Tyre, in 814 BCE. We do know its growing population stemmed from the sequence of Assyrian, Babylonian, and Persian attacks on the Phoenician cities along the eastern coast. These cities, especially Tyre and Sidon, had already established trading posts, which gradually became colonies, in Sicily, Sardinia, and along the Atlantic (Cadiz) and Mediterranean coast (Gibraltar to Malaga to Nerja) of Spain. The Cadiz connection was especially significant as it enabled the exchange of goods between Mesopotamia and the peoples along the Atlantic coast of Spain and France. Spain was particularly rich in tin, silver and gold. After the fall of Tyre, in 583, Carthage gradually became the *de facto* heir to these Phoenician colonies, and the new middleman for trade between the East and West! As Richard Harrison notes in <u>Spain at the Dawn of History</u>, there is a strong enough archaeological record about these colonial communities in Spain to explain the basis for Carthaginian power!

Rome is another example of the lack of an early historical record. Legend declares its founding in 753 BCE. Also, that it had seven kings before it became a Republic in 509 BCE, as a reaction to a particularly tyrannical ruler. There is little contemporary documentation from 1000 to 500 BCE to either establish or refute any of this!

While there are some helpful inscriptions after that time, significant surviving scribblings about Roman History or Culture must await Cicero in 61 BCE.

While both Rome and Carthage are described later as Republics, there is little to support such a claim before 500 BCE.

Greece is another matter! Thinking only about achievements in governance and culture, we can document that before 500 BCE citizens of Athens or other Greeks produced:

>750 BCE   A consensus date for the first written version of Homer's Epic poems, <u>Iliad</u> (the Trojan

War) and Odyssey (the post-war adventures of Odysseus.

MAP: Western Mediterranean

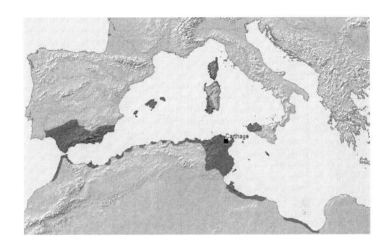

700 BCE   A similar date for Hesiod's Theogony and Works and Days. The first is about the relationships among Greek gods; the second about everyday life in Greece.

675-550   Two more Greek poets: Tyrtaeus of Sparta and Sappho produced works that survived.

594 BCE   Solon systemized the rules for Athenian Government.

585 BCE   Thales of Miletus successfully predicted a solar eclipse. This ultimately leads his followers to

become interested in both astronomy and philosophy which the Ancients believed were intimately related.

HOMER:

545-27 BCE   Pisistratus, an Athenian political leader, led the effort to certify the best Greek versions of Homer's Iliad and Odyssey. He also initiated the annual drama competition that motivated the comedy and tragic masterpieces of Euripides, Aeschylus, and Sophocles and Aristophanes.

509 BCE Athenians established a democracy in Athens. All propertied persons could vote, and leaders had to be re-elected annually.

Reflection: This is a lot! By 750 or so, Greece had already modified its Phoenician style alphabet to include vowels. These Greek vowels made narrative and literary writing less cumbersome and more reflective of what was heard. One Classics professor, Barry Powell, argues in Homer and the Origin of the Greek Alphabet (1991) that their vowel-powered alphabet was devised specifically for reading Homer's works. Whatever the motive, Greeks took the oral masterpieces already produced (Iliad, Odyssey, Theogony, and Works and Days) and converted them into written ones. Since they were written as poems, they could be more easily memorized and recited!

After 500 BCE, there will be prose narratives about both Persia and Greece. But, they will come from the Greek historians: Herodotus, Xenophon and Thucydides, who write in the 400's. Old Testament Books also provide sources, but not Persians.

We moderns may sniffle that the Athenian democracy of 509 excluded women, slaves and others, but if we pause to tour the neighborhood: it is a single bright ray in a night sky full of hereditary absolute power kingships. Also, it was a direct democracy, not merely a representative one. As such, they not only selected their leaders but themselves voted on such matters as: going to war or not, punishing its generals or not, and building a navy or reducing taxes! Despite grumbling elsewhere in Greece, the Athenian model of government would spread to other city-states in Greece and to several islands of the Aegean Sea. Athenians eventually also extended suffrage to unpropertied *thetes* and further limited the authority of elected leaders.

Iconic Event: In his book, The Rise of Athens (2016), Anthony Everitt discusses the accomplishments of the wise "tyrant" of Athens, Pisistratus (545-527 BCE), who embraced the cause of the landless *thetes* as well as Athenian cultural leadership of Greece. He is credited with promoting the public readings of Homer at the annual Panathenian Festival. Judges there awarded prizes for theater

GREEK THEATER

Performances at the annual Dionysian Festival that led to playwright excellence in the centuries that followed.

Chapter 4: THE AGE OF PERSIAN HEGEMONY, 500 to 338 BCE.

We know so much during this era about Greece and its Golden Age that it is easy to lose sight of the fact that Persia's political power was truly the dominant one!

Over these 160 years, **Persia** maintained the huge empire that Darius described on the Wall at Behistun. Until about 441 BCE, the Delian League, a group of city-states that Athens led, was a constant, but minor, concern for them. After that, Persian successor kings employed a divide-and-conquer strategy in dealing with Greeks. Athen's naval and cultural success had, meanwhile, inflamed the jealousies of other major Greek city states such as Sparta, Corinth and Thebes. Persians shrewdly exploited these Greek rivalries, intervening to assist one side or the other (usually Sparta). Persian thumbs were often on the scales during the Second Peloponnesian war, from 431 to 401 BCE: a civil war where Greeks decimated one another! It reached the peak of its influence in 386 when King Artaxerxes mediated, and agreed to help Sparta enforce, a treaty between Sparta and Athens in exchange for their acknowledging Persian hegemony over previously independent Greek cities. *(for more detail about these wars, see Appendix #1)*.

In the east, Persian kings more or less successfully managed revolts and administrative matters in Babylon and Egypt where so much more wealth was at stake. We do know they lost effective control of Egypt for the 53 years from 401 to 348 BCE, but did re-establish dominance there from then to 338 BCE. So, by that time,

Egypt was back in the fold and Athens, their traditional nemesis, was on the ropes, due to losses from the Peloponnesian Wars.

Viewing this empire solely from our gold panning perspective of governing style and cultural heritage, the inheritances from Persia at this time for the west are disappointing. Politically, a single dynasty, the Achaemenids, ruled the Empire during this entire era. The emperor was a hereditary, absolute power, kingship. Most new kings had to purge relatives in order to secure their crown. Their religion was monotheistic, but tolerated other deities. Israelites seemed to prefer the Persians to either Babylonians or Neo-Assyrians.

The cultural legacy for the West is equally weak! The Persian Empire was the largest and wealthiest Mediterranean Empire to this point. Matt Waters' 2014 book, <u>Ancient Persia</u>, notes, though, that most of what we know about it came from fifth century or later Greeks; books of the Old Testament; and, to a lesser extent, clay tablets in libraries of places they conquered, and inscriptions found on their own palaces and tombs. There are some important exceptions: the Behistun Wall engravings, a clay cylinder about Cyrus the Great, and a find of thousands of clay tablets near Persepolis. While these items shed a light on some administrative practices, Persian records so far provide too little for a narrative of their political history. Nor is there a corresponding trove of surviving new literature such as the <u>Book of the Dead</u> or the <u>Gilgamesh Epic</u>.

While Persia dominated the East, two other nations with very different stories, were flowering in the West.

The years from 500 to 338 BCE were prosperous ones for **Carthage.** Persian conquest of the ports along the eastern Mediterranean led to a consolidation of Phoenician peoples into Carthage and its colonies. Few Carthaginian records survive, but those of other civilizations show Carthage had active colonies in Sicily, Sardinia and Spain. Aristotle admired their Republic for its stability: it allowed for assemblies to express popular thinking; two annually elected *suffetes* (similar to Roman consuls) for actual governing; and a Council of 300 to debate and recommend policy.

From Greek sources, we know Carthage, in 479 BCE, failed in its effort to establish a colony on Sicily. Then, in 413, its navy decisively defeated Athens when the democracy tried to assist its own colony there. The Athens loss was a disaster that marked a turning point against them in the Peloponnesian war.

This military decline of Greece opened up the Western Mediterranean to both Carthage and Rome. Up to this point, these two powers had avoided conflict with one another: Rome had no Navy; they signed treaties of Alliance with Carthage in both 348 and 302.

Roman historians traditionally date 509 BCE as the start of their Republic. For want of contrary evidence, many modern scholars accept this! Mary Beard, though, in her recent book on Rome, SPQR, makes a persuasive case that the Republic came more gradually and might not have begun until 367 BCE when the register of the list of names of consuls first used the term "consul" instead of "colonel".

Future archaeological finds might provide a clearer answer. In the meantime, all parties concede that by mid 300s Rome was a Republic with a senate, an active assembly for popular input, and two annually elected consuls. The consuls could succeed themselves only in emergencies and had to agree on domestic policy and lead their armies. She also notes that the earliest inscriptions are in a Latin form that resembles Greek, complete with vowels.

By 340 BCE, Rome only controlled an area 90 miles long and 30 miles wide, and, by 300, had between 60,000 and 90,000 people. As yet, they had produced no literature or historical narratives of their own: the first two Roman historians were Fabius *Pictor*, who wrote in about 200 BCE, and *Cato the Elder* (234-149 BCE). Also, by 350, Rome was 90 years from building a navy.

Reflection: Looking solely for our cultural and political inheritance, and solely outside Greece, there is rather little to jot down in our notebooks as to cultural heritage. But, governmentally, both Rome and Carthage are republics with governing systems designed to restrain tyrants. They have separate senates (drawn from among landed aristocrats), assemblies (providing for a popular voice), and executives elected by one or the other! Given what has gone before and occurs elsewhere in the region, this is a big deal!

Iconic Event: The signing of the King's Peace in 386 both illustrates and symbolizes the influence of Persia during this era. The treaty itself begins with, "I, Artaxerxes, consider it just…" He later threatens to make

war on anyone who does not accept the treaty terms. It was a humiliation for all Greeks. As Jennifer Roberts notes in <u>Plague of War</u>, this would backfire against Sparta as other Greek cities would blame them for giving so much to Persia. It would also spur Isocrates, a famous orator, to repeatedly and relentless call upon Greek cities to unite and invade Persia! Which they ultimately did!

Chapter 5: GREECE AND MACEDONIA, 500 to 338 BCE

The Greek Classical Age:

The military story of Greece in this era is colorfully told in Jennifer Roberts', <u>The Plague of War</u>, 2017. In summary: Athens led a defensive coalition that defeated the Persians in 490 BCE. After that attack, the people wisely voted to invest the proceeds from a nearby silver mine to build a navy. With the new navy, Athens both defeated the Persians in 480 and in subsequent decades. Their navy brought them great power that made other Greeks jealous and, perhaps, made themselves arrogant. The resulting Peloponnesian Wars from 458 to 401 and weakened all Greeks by 338 BCE.

Athens also embraced a democratic approach to governance! Most of its allies in the Delian League that Athens led also practiced democratic values with large numbers allowed to vote in their own assemblies. Some undocumented earlier experience apparently led all Greeks to fear a tyrant. Even conservative Sparta had two kings with a council that chose which would lead them for the next year!

Other Greek city-states favored oligarchy, where only a limited number (10-20) of aristocrats had a voice in decisions. In Athens, and many of its allies, even lower class *thetes* who often served as rowers on warships had full voting rights in the Assembly.

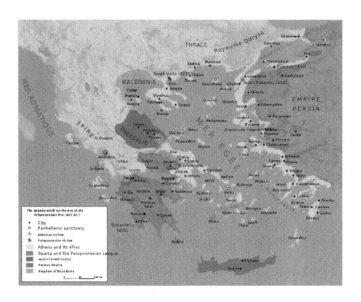

To further prevent a tyrant, Athenian democracy included leadership by ten popularly elected "generals"; the right of the assembly to vote on key decisions, and the opportunity to "ostracize ", or exile for ten years, any person the majority thought disruptive to good order. Though slaves, women, and the unpropertied could not vote in the Assembly, those who could vote were very influential, casting votes on many crucial decisions.

While Athenian leadership in promoting democracy is unique and important, the legacy of the art, literature, and science, that it, and other Greek cities, produced had the most permanent impact.

One very noticeable cultural change is that three individuals wrote histories of their own and of earlier times, giving us a window and level of color and detail that was previously unavailable. Writing in 440 BCE,

Herodotus traveled throughout all of Persia and reported his impressions of their culture and history. Inspired by him, *Thucydides* and *Xenophon* wrote 35 years later, giving accounts of wars they actually participated in. Much of what we know about the politics and wars of this period is from them.

Consider also the volume and quality of the cultural and scientific writings that survived:

Literature: City funding of the Dionysus Festival in Athens led to the production and preservation of the works of many of the magnificent plays and playwrights of the era. *Aeschylus, Sophocles, Euripides,* and *Aristophanes* produced 45 surviving plays out of over 400 that they wrote. They will not be matched until the 1500s CE. Some of the better known are listed below:

Aeschylus was the first great tragedian. Only 7 of his 70 plays survive, including The Persians (472 BCE), and the trilogy, Oresteia (458).

Sophocles produced 123 plays, of which 7 survive to the present, including Antigone (441 BCE) and Oedipus Rex (431).

Euripides had the most plays survive: 19 of his 92 plays did so, among them: Medea, (431 BCE) and The Trojan Women (415).

Aristophanes wrote comedies rather than tragedies from 425 to 388 BCE including: Clouds, Frogs, and Lysistrata. Twelve of his 40 works survive.

These four writers endured over the next several centuries, and their works are still performed, even providing the plots for several twentieth century motion pictures!

Rhetoric: Public speaking and persuasion, known then as rhetoric, was an important skill in the political and legal arenas because Greece was a democracy. *Corax,* a Greek from Syracuse, another democracy, was the first to write about the principles of rhetoric, sometime in the fifth century BCE. *Isocrates*, though, established the first School of Rhetoric (436-338). *Aristotle* built on that, however, with Rhetoric, in three volumes, written sometime between 335 and 332; this became the standard text.

Sculpture and Architecture: Mesopotamian and Egyptian civilizations produced striking buildings and statuary. The Greeks of this period also left impressive sculptures and public structures; the statues were notably more lifelike, and the buildings reflected Greek mastery of the principles of artistic perspective.

One prime example is Kritios Boy, a bronze sculpture traditionally used to mark the beginning of the Classical Era (480 BCE). It is lifelike and demonstrates the artist's correct understanding of how the parts of the body work as a system.

The sculptor and architect *Phidias* is connected with many the marvelous achievements of the Age:

He designed and rebuilt the Parthenon, including its sculptures and pediments, 447-438 BCE. The columns are sized at slightly different widths to achieve visual perspective.

He produced a 38 foot masterpiece made of gold and ivory for the Parthenon, Athena Parthenos, the symbol of Athens, 447-438 BCE.

Phidias also created the 42 foot high statue of Zeus at the Temple in Olympia, also of gold and ivory, one of the Seven Wonders of the Ancient World. (See **icon** below).

Praxilites was the leading sculptor from 358 to 330. There is an extant example of his work, Aphrodite of Cnidius. He worked with marble and was famed for full-sized nude females.

Medicine, Science, Math: Tradition names *Hippocrates* as the author of the 60-plus medicine-related texts dated between 430 to 330 BCE. Topics include epilepsy, treating the whole person, a scientific approach, and famously "doing no harm". *Democritus* (490-460) was also a physician. He was the first to posit that all things were made up of invisible and indivisible atoms. His theory was the starting point not only for medical understanding but also for much ancient philosophy and modern science (after microscopes confirmed he was correct). *Aristotle,* famous as a philosopher, also wrote extensively about the natural world.

Philosophy: Two of the Greek thinkers of this era are so important that their competing views of man and his relationship with God and the natural world are the starting points for most such future discussions! A central theme is man's continuing effort to understand the universe and whether he should even try to.

Plato, a student of Socrates, lived from 396-347. He is most noted for his argument that material reality is unknowable and illusional. All reality is ultimately spiritual. His influence on subsequent philosophers was enormous, and early Christian theologians usually embraced him.

Aristotle was active from 367 to 331. His writings ranged from logic and rhetoric to mathematics and science. They include some books on Natural Philosophy that explored the nature of the universe. He advocated studying all aspects of the natural world, arguing that the material world is knowable **and** that a combination of reason and our senses suffice to prove the existence of both God and the spiritual world.

Reflection: To me, it's clear that these 160 years in Greece marked a huge creative outburst in both governmental style and cultural and literary output (*For additional details on the Playwrights and Sculpture, see Endnote # 5)*. It stands out starkly compared with either previous empires or with those of its own age. But, could it survive the constant warfare and destruction around it? These were fragile writings and the growing weakness among the Greek city-states augured poorly.

Iconic Event: Below is an artistic interpretation of the majesty of Phidias' massive Statue of Zeus at Olympia. Here, he demonstrates key features of the Classic Era such

PHIDIAS: STATUE OF ZEUS:

as a lifelike appearance and an understanding of linear perspective.

Macedonia Rising:

Prior to 359 BCE, we know little about Macedonia except that it was a weak kingdom whose amorphous borders varied over time depending on the results of wars with its five neighbors. Its royalty was Greek in culture and language. Scholars are still arguing about the ethnicity (or Greekness) of the populace. From Persian administrative records, we know it was a longtime subordinate ally of the Empire.

Philip II of Macedon became King in 358 after his brother was killed in battle. From Greek sources, we know Phillip loved Hellenic learning and culture and spent two formative years as a hostage in Thebes, Greece. He hired Aristotle to educate his son, Alexander! By 357, he pacified or conquered his five neighbors and eliminated other claimants to the throne.

Several factors underlay Phillip's success! One was the discovery of gold on nearby Mount Pangaeus: gold fueled his purchase and training of mercenaries. Second, he used more lightly armored and mobile troops, armed with unusually long 13-foot spears. They could kill enemies well before the latter's weapons could be brought into play. Lastly, Greece was looking for a hero to unite them! A famous teacher, writer, and speaker, *Isocrates* of Athens, had been advocating for over 40 years, and persuading some, that Greeks should unite in a "holy war" against Persia to avenge the destruction of Athens in 480! More recently, *Isocrates* wrote his <u>Philippics</u>, in 346, specifically pointing to Phillip as the one to lead the Greeks.

Philip and his 20 year old son Alexander moved south to invade Greece with 30,000 men in 338 and, at Chaeronea, decisively defeated a coalition that included Athens and Thebes. Alexander led the left flank that decisively crushed the Thebans! As terms of surrender, Philip shrewdly offered the Athenians an Alliance - which they accepted. This gave him a navy and access to Athenian colonies on the Dardanelles! He then formed a League of Corinth consisting of 30 Greek states that pledged to invade Persia.

The Twisty Trail

Chapter 6: HELLENISTIC ERA IN THE EAST, 338 to 146 BCE.

The Fall of Persia:

In 336 BCE, Philip was assassinated at the Macedonian capital. Some contended that Alexander's mother was behind it; Alexander blamed the Persians. After quelling a rebellion in Thebes, a powerful city in central Greece, he moved his force of 40,000 infantry and 7000 cavalry across the Hellespont to Asia. His army met and defeated the much larger Persian forces at the Granicus River in northwest Anatolia in 334.

Over the next thirteen years, he won three other battles over the Persians, founded the city of Alexandria in Egypt, took over the Persian Empire after Darius was killed by his own men, won other battles in India, and died in Babylon in 323. (*See Appendix #2 for more details on Alexander's Campaigns*).

After Alexander's death, though, his top lieutenants murdered his family and relatives, and fought one another over his Empire. The upshot, by 305 BCE, was that Ptolemy, governor of Egypt, retained Egypt, Libya and the Levant; Seleucus controlled Mesopotamia and Persia; Antigonas Gonatus claimed Macedonia and Greece. After a time, a fourth empire developed in the Greek city of Pergamum, located in Central Asia Minor (241 BCE).

The fate of these empires varied! The Ptolemies, from their new great city, Alexandria, governed Egypt until the death of Cleopatra in 30 BCE. The Seleucid Empire, with Antioch, (Syria), as its capital, lasted until 64 BCE, but was already much reduced in size and influence once the Parthians of Persia gained their independence by 138 . The Macedonian empire proved the shortest. In 168 BCE, Rome broke it up into four Republics and in 148 made it into a mere province. Pergamum was independent only from 263 to 133 BCE.

Cultural Legacy in the East:

Alexander is mostly known for the size of his empire and his tactical and strategic brilliance! This brought him little: his dynasty lasted only nine years, compared with the nearly 200 year Empire that Cyrus the Great established. Then, it broke into three or four mini Empires - none with democratic practices. But, they were all Greek and very proud of their heritage. As it happened, one of his, and their, lasting achievements was the preservation and expansion of the great cultural outburst of the Classical Age that Alexander and Philip respected so much. A second was that vowel-based Greek, for the next 200 years, became the language of diplomacy for the entire East.

Whatever their other faults, the heirs to his Empire were Greek and shared a love for Greek culture, and they showed it in several ways:

They sponsored "Dionysian Artists", a traveling troupe of actors and others to perform the great Greek tragedies and comedies under Royal protection throughout the Hellenistic Empires.

They also sponsored the construction of libraries to store what knowledge humans had so far achieved. While the Great Library of Alexandria (est. 306 BCE) was the most famous, others were built in primary cities like Athens, Antioch and Pergamum. The one in Alexandria, with over 500,000 scrolls committed to collect a copy of every extant book. (*See Appendix #4 for more details on these libraries*).

But the writers of the Hellenistic Era also added to the roster of great ancient writings. A complete list and description of these is beyond the scope of this essay, but consider:

<u>History</u>: We know of many history writers during this era, but only the writings of *Polybius (*200 to 118 BCE), a Greek who lived in Rome, survived past the middle ages. His <u>Histories</u> reflects his knowledge of both cultures and is mainly about Rome and the Punic (Carthaginian) Wars,

<u>Theater</u>: *Menander* (342-292 BCE) wrote over 100 comedies. Romans loved them. The Roman playwright *Plautus* (254-184) famously adapted and translated them for the Roman ear. Eight are recorded as winners in the

annual Athens Dionysian Competition. All but one has since been lost.

Philosophy: *Epicurus* (342-241 BCE) and *Zeno* (335-263 BCE) each developed new philosophies that helped followers cope with the new Greek world of lost independence. Both built upon the theory of *Democritus* (490-460 BCE) that all things are composed of invisible and indivisible atoms. None of Epicurus's work survives, but it is persuasively presented years later by the Roman, *Lucretius* (99-55 BCE), in On the Nature of Things.

Sculpture: In Alexander the Great's view, Lysippus was the greatest sculptor of the period and allowed only him to portray his likeness. While no originals survive, Romans made many copies and sometimes placed their own face on the Lysippus pose.

Medicine and Science: By 300 BCE, doctors were already dissecting corpses to understand the human nerves and other body systems. About the same year, *Euclid* wrote his geometry textbook, Elements, the standard for centuries. *Archimedes* (287-212), the greatest mathematician of the Age, wrote On the Measurement of the Circle, calculated the value of *pi,* and established the foundations for calculus. *Aristarchus* (310-230) recorded data showing that the planets Mars and Venus revolve around the sun, not the Earth. His "heliocentric" theory of the universe meant the earth went around the sun as well. *Hipparchus* (190-126) laid out the locations of over 850 stars and developed a system for predicting solstices and eclipses.

Alexandria was the center of these scientific discoveries in the Hellenistic world. Most of its findings went unchallenged until the Renaissance.

Reflection: What would be the fate of Greek learning if Persia had conquered Macedonia and Greece rather than the reverse? As it happened, Greek learning was not only preserved, but promoted and expanded. Use of the Greek language spread throughout the region and, by 146 BCE, was the primary language of diplomacy or scholarship. The speakers of other languages, such as Hebrew, Latin, and Arabic, came to appreciate the importance of vowels, and added them to their own writing systems.

I also note that the bulk of the new work on mathematics, science and astronomy occurs in the East, particularly Alexandria. These sciences are all more interrelated than I realized. Astronomy was critical to obtaining an understanding of the ancient universe. Night travel and stars were important in the hot shifting sands of the desert. Without astronomy, solstices, eclipses and planetary movements were just random events caused by the whims of the gods. Geometry, geography, and trigonometry enabled the precise calculations needed to develop an accurate calendar and forecast movements in the skies. Together, these could make our world more understandable and rational.

Iconic Event: For me, the traveling **Dionysian Artists** convey the spirit or zeitgeist of the Age in the East. All three empires in the wake of Alexander were committed to Greek culture and this is one activity that united them!

DIONYSIUS FESTIVAL:

Chapter 7: HELLENISTIC INFLUENCE IN THE WEST, 338 to 146 BCE.

The Duel over the West:

In the first seventy years after 338, three Western power centers, all republics, were flourishing. By 265 BCE, **Rome** had gradually unified its Peninsula; it had good relations with the Greek cities there, and an alliance treaty with Carthage. Its primary concern was the unpredictable behavior of the Celts on its northern border. Less is known about **Carthage,** other than that it too was thriving and looking for more colonies in Sicily. The third power, **Syracuse**, on the isle of Sicily, was the most influential, independent, Greek city. Sicily was an important grain source for Rome.

Then in 265 BCE, some Italian mercenaries unexpectedly let Pandora out of her box: they captured and garrisoned the Greek city of Messana (modern Messina), which overlooks the narrow straits separating Sicily and Italy. Syracuse was outraged, but unable to re-capture the city by itself, so one faction appealed to Carthage and another to Rome. Carthage quickly voted to help and soon occupied the city. The Roman Senate wanted to stay out and voted accordingly. But Rome's Assembly, persuaded by the consuls who feared Carthaginian control of the Straits, overruled the Senate (for the first time ever recorded). Carthage -still a Roman ally- turned the garrison over to Rome, but then formed a new alliance with Syracuse. The

First Punic War was on!

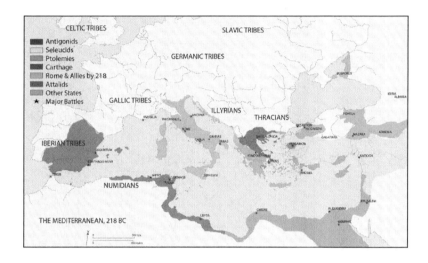

MAP OF WESTERN MEDITERRANEAN:

A major turning point in Roman History came five years later in 260 BCE. They built a navy! They did so because they could not defend any of their allies on Sicily without one. So they constructed 100 quatrimenes (larger but slower than the Carthaginian and Greek triremes). They added a large gangway that could be dropped in a timely manner to facilitate boarding of other ships with Roman troops. For the next 18 years, the two fleets battered one another until 242. Carthage, with no more ships left to protect its allies, agreed to a peace where they ceded Sicily, Sardinia, and Corsica to the Romans, leaving them only with Further and Nearer Spain.

The Second Punic War (218-212) features Hannibal's crossing of the Alps, annihilating a series of Roman Armies, but still unable to win the war! Unfortunately for Macedonia, its king had helped Hannibal and so, when the war was over, Rome sent a punitive expedition to Macedonia and, in 197 BCE, destroyed the Macedonian army.

In the following year, the victorious general, Flamininus, went to Athens for an Olympic Event and told the Greeks he wanted them to be independent--Rome did not want provinces, only allies. Greeks greeted this with much support and enthusiasm. Similarly, the Roman Senate said they did not want to rule Carthage directly. These turn-of-the-century Romans were ambivalent about becoming an Empire. While they made Sicily, Corsica, Sardinia and Spain into provinces, they preferred a more subtle relationship with the republics of Carthage, Greece and with Macedonia.

Over the next 50 years, though, the Kings of Macedonia and of the Seleucid Empire flexed their muscles in an effort to restore the glories of their ancient kingdoms. Rome responded to these threats, and decisively defeated the Seleucids (Antioch) in 190 and Macedonia in 168 BCE. In that same year, Rome showed its power by making Macedonia a province and forcing the Seleucids to abandon their effort to conquer a vulnerable Egypt.

In 146 BCE, Rome dealt with perceived insurrections in Greece and Carthage which led to the defeat of each, and the razing of both Carthage and Corinth, the wealthiest city in Greece. Rome was now the military Master of the Mediterranean!

Hellenistic Culture in Rome:

Greek culture spread throughout the East Mediterranean due to the conquest by Alexander and, more importantly, the Greek dynasties that governed the area for the next two centuries; by contrast, it flourished in the West because Greece and Macedonia were conquered and plundered by a Roman elite who also admired their cultural achievements. Roman taste for Greek histories, literature, sculptures, and rhetoric is what would ensure the preservation of a joint Greco-Roman culture for the next 500 years.

History: *Fabius Pictor*, the first known Roman-born historian, wrote in Greek in about 200 BCE. None of his work survived to the Middle Ages, but Polybius, Livy, and Dionysius all relied on him. *Polybius* (200 BCE to 118), the second important historian for this era, was a Greek-born slave to a wealthy Roman. He wrote a Histories of Rome that focused on the Punic Wars. Cato the Elder (234-149) wrote Origines, the first Roman history by a Roman in Latin (168 BCE).

Literature: Rome produced two important playwrights: both were Greek inspired! *Plautus* (254-185 BCE) was a Roman who adapted many of Menander's plays to a Roman audience. *Terence* (195-159 BCE) was a Greek-born hostage who wrote six surviving original comedies that were in a Greek style.

Plunder also spread Greek literature and culture. When Aemilius Paullus defeated the Macedonian king Perseus in 168 BCE, he brought back the entire Royal Library as booty,

Art and sculpture: Once again, booty is an important means of cultural transmission. When Marcellus conquered the Greek city, Syracuse, in 212 BCE, he brought back many statues and other marvelous artistic pieces, adorned many public places in Rome, and, according to Plutarch, opened the eyes of elites and plebes to the wonders and subtleties of Greek art.

Much later, in 146 BCE, Roman general Lucius Mummius took the time to sack all the valuables of wealthy Corinth and send them to Rome, before levelling Corinth to the ground.

Philosophy: Rome was initially less enthusiastic about philosophy than in other Greek skills. In 155 BCE, a group of leading Athenian philosophers visited Rome. While the initial reception was lukewarm, Rome would go on to build on the Greeks and produce many thoughtful thinkers of their own.

Reflection: How real was the Greek impact on Roman Culture? One persuasive bit of evidence is from the Roman senator, Cato the Elder, 234-149 BCE. Cato lived up to his curmudgeon *persona*, mainly by calling for both the total destruction of Carthage and for resistance to Greek influence. He clearly thought Greek ideas were pervasive and corrupting. Even so, he made sure his son had a Greek teacher.

Cato would likely mourn, but concede, that Chester Starr in his <u>The Ancient World</u> is accurate in observing that the Romans were "amazingly receptive" to Greek culture and, by 133 BCE, were comfortable (Cato would say "too comfortable") in the literary, artistic and intellectual world of Hellenistic culture.

Iconic Event: I think the sacking of Syracuse, a Greek city, in 212, is a good symbol for the spread of Greek culture in this Hellenistic Period. When Marcellus

brought back to Rome the marvelous art and sculptures he found there as booty, he put the wonders of Greek Art into sharp focus. He used many such items to decorate public parts of the city. It reminds me how important looting was to inspiring the Roman admiration of things Greek. And how important the Roman role was to the survival of Classical wonders.

The Twisty Trail

Chapter 8: BIRTH PANGS OF THE EMPIRE, 146 BCE to 60 BCE.

As of 146 BCE, Rome was the dominant force in the entire Mediterranean. In the West, all of North Africa from Carthage to the Gates of Hercules; to Further to Nearer Spain; to the islands of Sardinia, Corsica and Sicily; and even to Greece and Macedonia: all were provinces under the thumb of Rome. In the East, its dominance stemmed mostly from its military reputation and its alliances. At this point, though, the eastern kingdoms clearly deferred to Rome's dominant influence.

From a governance perspective, the toppling of Greece and Carthage meant Rome was the only remaining Republic in the east or west. A closer look though discloses that it was not a "balanced" Republic with an effective voice for the both the popular Assembly and the aristocratic Senate. The actual workings of the Republic from 146 to 60 BCE display something closer to one party rule. It also discloses patterns of corruption and political greed that foreshadow the collapse of the Republic that followed in the forties.

Cicero, 100-44, writing after 61 BCE, is the first observer to comment on this era. He looks back several generations later and describes a split in Roman thinking between the *'optimares'* (better people, landed aristocrats) in the Senate, and the *'populares'* (found more often in the popular assembly). He and some like-minded others who wrote a bit later portray 146-105 BCE as an ideal time when, with one or two aberrations, the people respected

Senatorial leadership. The aberrations, they admit, were significant. They included slave insurrections in Sicily; the complete corruption of Senators by a Numidian King, Jugurtha, and the Senate's brazen murder of the *populare* leader, Gaius Gracchus, in 133. Twelve years later, Senate aristocrats also murdered his brother Tiberius and massacred over 300 of his supporters.

This slaughter of their opposition produced unbroken *optimare* control and Senate dominance for a generation until the army of the Republic faced a crisis in 105 BCE in confronting a threat from a huge Celtic tribe to their northern borders.

Beginning of the End:

Michael Duncan's The Storm before the Storm (2018) describes the land reforms and food programs the Gracci brothers promoted, their assassinations, and the eventual adoption of their proposed reforms. Scholars still argue whether aristocratic purchase of land from small landholders was itself the primary cause of the land distribution problem. Increasing the number of landholders was very important to the army as only landowners could be soldiers.

Duncan also highlights the importance of the crisis of 105 BCE that arrived in the wake of huge Roman battlefield losses to the Cimbri, a Celtic tribe! Years earlier, the senate had sent two different *optimare*-supported generals against them, and each army had been decimated. Then, after still another slaughter at Arausio in 105 BCE and the loss of 80,000 more men, a desperate senate appointed Gaius Marius, a successful *populare* general, as consul. They even provided him with rarely offered extensions to his one year term. Due to growing manpower shortages, they also awarded him the authority to recruit soldiers from among the landless classes. (*For details about the Cimbri Wars, see Appendix 4*).

Once Marius (157-86 BCE) defeated this threat, he was promptly honored as a Third Founder of Rome. His grateful country elected him twice more as consul: two consecutive terms during peacetime, in violation of past standards. His primary political interests at first seemed limited. As his mostly unpropertied troops were without homesteads, he wanted to reward them, both Italians and Romans, with land to retire in. Second, as he was himself an Italian, he wanted Italians to have fair representation in the Assembly.

Over the next few years, though, Marius and his *populare* political allies not only allocated land in Gaul for his troops, but also enacted measures that restricted Senate power and expanded the role of the Assembly.

The tipping point came in 91 BCE and the Wheel of Fortune took another turn! The *optimare* regained power and firmly rejected full citizenship for the Italians, even though these Italians made up a very large portion of the Army they all depended upon for protection. Romans, whether landed aristocrats or urban workers, refused to share power with their allies in the rest of Italy.

To Roman surprise, the Italians revolted. The subsequent War against the Allies, 91-88 BCE, was a very bloody affair that cost the Empire 300,000 men, further draining its future manpower. Even after a reluctant *optimare* Senate agreed to award fair suffrage to the Italians, the battles lingered on. Lucius Sulla was the general who brought victory finally to Rome in 88 BCE, the same year that the Senate exiled Marius.

Next, the Senate rewarded Sulla by sending him off to Greece to collect his army and deal with problems in Asia Minor. While he was in transit, the Assembly cancelled Sulla's appointment and gave it to Marius. So, Marius returned to Italy from his exile, raised an army, and captured a supportive Rome. He was named consul for the seventh time, but then ordered a hideous massacre of hundreds of his enemies, including three of the *optimare* leaders that had ordered his banishment. He died two years later.

Mithridates, Sulla and Pompey, 88-63 BCE: Meanwhile, Sulla took his army east to attend to Mithridates the Great, king of Pontus (120-63 BCE). The king had successfully built a powerful Empire along the entire circumference of the Black Sea, including Crimea and Byzantium, as well as, by 90 BCE, most of Anatolia (modern Turkey).

When Mithridates interfered with a Roman ally, Bithynia, the Senate sent an army to assist the Bithynians. The great King then declared war in 88 BCE and shattered the Roman forces so completely he was able to conquer all the rest of Anatolia, the Greek cities along the the Aegean shore, and the kingdom of Pergamum. He also sent an army to Athens and obtained their submission. Then, Mithridates ordered the massacre of all Italians and Romans in Asia Minor, about 80,000 persons.

When Sulla learned the Roman Assembly and tribune had revoked his command of the Eastern Army, he marched his army on Rome instead. Once there, he changed his mind and turned east with the army and outfought Mithridates in a series of battles in 86 and 85. In the latter year, Mithridates signed the Treaty of the Dardanelles, agreeing to give up all his recent conquests.

Meanwhile, Marius died. With Mithridates defeated, a triumphant Sulla took his army back to Rome to deal with his enemies there! He expected a hostile reception as the *populares* still controlled Rome. *Populares* favored full parity for Italian allies in citizenship and suffrage which was very popular in Southern Italy; the *optimares* did not. Also, Sulla had been the leading general, fighting the Italians, in the War against the Allies not so long ago. He had slaughtered 6,000 defenseless Italian Samnites in Rome after promising them they would only be sold into slavery!

Shrewdly, Sulla landed his army at Brindisi, on the heel of Italy, and announced he now favored full parity for Italians. He also stressed a peaceful intent to punish only a few leading enemies. Opposition melted away as he slowly moved north to Rome. When he reached it, he kept his promise on the Italian issue; but he ordered a bloodbath against the *populare*. As a result, 3000 of them were killed; including 100 *populare* Senators. No previous Roman purge of enemies, and there were several, was as bloody as this.

Next, Sulla reversed all previous *populare* legislation; increased the Senate from 300 to 600 members (appointing 400); ordered the exhuming and dishonoring of Marius's ashes; and had himself appointed dictator. Few of Marius's kin would survive. One who did was his nephew, Gaius Julius Caesar. Sulla's supporters note their hero died a natural death, but his detractors allege he was eaten alive by worms in 78 BCE after he had retired to write his memoirs (which very regrettably, do not survive).

Meanwhile, Mithridates continued to rule his much smaller empire and annoy Rome for the next 20 years, winning a few victories along the way. In 66 BCE, the Senate appointed Pompey the Great to take over the Roman army in Asia Minor. After several defeats, Mithridates committed suicide in 63 BCE and sent his own head to a victorious Pompey.

Reflection: I agree that Michael Duncan's Storm before the Storm set the table for the Crisis that followed in the forties. Before the Cimbri War, the Army only allowed propertied persons to man their legions; they already had land so did not need some for their retirement. The Cimbri victories caused a severe manpower crisis and, under Marius, now depended upon the landless recruit. This made the Republic vulnerable to any successful general who was more loyal to his soldiers than to Senate aristocrats.

Second, Sulla's bloody purge of *populares* would not be forgotten. When another crisis came in the forties, the Wheel of Fortune would turn against the Republic. On the upside, Romans then produced a Golden Age of Culture and Literature of their own.

Iconic Event: Sulla's Dictatorship is the most emblematic event of this dismal time. His bloodbath against his enemies, within two generations, would be reciprocated against his beloved *optimares*; his anti-Assembly reforms would be reversed within a decade; his painstakingly written memoir would be lost.

REIGN OF SULLA:

Chapter 9: BIRTH OF THE EMPIRE, 60 BCE to 18 CE.

Sulla's dictatorship, new constitutional changes, and the massacre of *populare* opposition left *optimares* and the Senate in firm control of the Empire. After his death in 78 BCE, his two primary lieutenants, Crassus and Pompey, were both *optimares* leaders. Even so, by 70, when they were the two consuls, they nonetheless dismantled most of Sulla's reforms in order to increase their own popularity in the Assembly.

As of 60 BCE, Pompey, victor over Mithridates, was already established as a successful military figure; Crassus, a very wealthy man, was a political power, but one who still needed the prestige that only an independent military victory could bring. While Gaius Julius Caesar had a record of military success in Spain, he was in debt, mainly to Crassus. Caesar was also a *populare* leader and a nephew of their hero, Marius. He would need votes from *optimare* allies in the senate.

To accomplish each of their goals, the three agreed to cooperate rather than fight!

The Triumvirate, 60-49 BCE: Accordingly, the senate enabled Crassus to raise an army against the Parthians, who had recently conquered Syria. They also supported Caesar's election as consul and authorized him to take his legions to Gaul where he could, if successful, plunder the

Gauls and pay off his debts. Pompey would stay in Rome to handle the Senate. In 62, he had already disbanded his successful army that subdued Mithridates, and he wanted Senate and Assembly approval to find a place to settle his veterans.

While a very sensible scheme, republican purists muttered because tradition forbade consuls from serving two consecutive years. Caesar would ultimately serve nine successive and largely lucrative years in Gaul. Crassus's tenure would also be extended until 53 BCE so he could raise and move his army to the Euphrates where, in that year, he, and it, would be ambushed and slaughtered at Carrhae.

Civil War, 49-31 BCE: Just before Caesar's term expired in 49 BCE, Pompey broke with him and allied himself with Senators who wanted to recall and prosecute Julius. *Optimares* grumbled that Caesar had used his army to enrich himself and slaughter over 1,000,000 Gauls. Caesar could only be legally protected from prosecution while he served as consul. So, on the one hand, the Senate's biggest worry for the Republic was a popular general like Marius or Caesar; but, on the other, any general asked now to lay aside his army would surely consider the fate of Marius and his followers when exposed to the tender mercies of a Sulla and an *optimare* Senate.

So Caesar famously crossed the Rubicon with his legions! Within a year, he captured Rome (after Pompey retreated to Macedonia) **and** captured Spain, Sardinia and Sicily.

Then, in 47, with only 24,000 men, he met and destroyed Pompey's 47,000 veterans at Pharsalus in Macedonia. Pompey fled to Egypt where he was betrayed and killed. Caesar next led his army across Asia Minor and defeated Pharnaces, the son of Mithridates. His armies followed this up with decisive victories against the remaining Roman forces in Africa in 46 and Spain in 45. This was the entire known Mediterranean world, except Persia and India.

Caesar Then returned to Rome to obtain, from an intimidated Senate, the needed legal protections for himself. He also secured an authorization to lead an army against the Parthians who so embarrassed Rome at Carrhae. The Senate voted him his commission and **a dictatorship for life**, but, on March 15 44 BCE, a group of about 20 senators stabbed him to death.

In the wake of this, Lepidus, Marc Antony (Caesar's top lieutenant) and Octavian (Caesar's adopted son) formed a second triumvirate against the forces of the *optimare* Senators. After Lepidus died in battle, Octavian and Antony, in 43, launched a proscription (massacre) of their opponents, including Cicero. They executed 300 senators and over 2000 other optimare leaders. This effectively liquidated the Republic. They also divided the Empire into two; the West to Octavian; the East to Antony.

The final act came 12 years later at the naval Battle of Actium (near Corinth) in 31 BCE. Within a few months, Antony was dead and Octavian was Emperor.

*Augustus, 31 BCE- 14 CE (*Common Era *aka* Anno Domino, AD*)*: Octavian became 'Augustus' and led the Empire for 45 years. He provided a stability that Rome maybe never experienced before. Over time, he solidified the boundaries of the Roman state to include the rest of North Africa, Spain, Gaul, and even Parthia. After an ambush and massacre of three legions in Germany's Teutoburg Forest in 9 BCE, he set a northern limit for the Empire at the Rhine and Danube Rivers.

Gradually, the power of the Assembly dissolved; the Senate role nominally increased, but was largely limited to provincial administration, leading legions, and advice. The Emperor gained control over the Army by appointing its generals. He also gained Army loyalty by taking

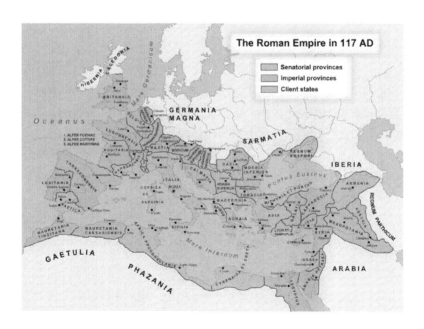

responsibility for rewarding veterans with land or with cash grants.

Augustus also provided important cultural leadership for the Empire. He authorized many building programs to convert a city of clay into one of marble. These include the Pantheon. Further, when Virgil wrote the Aeneid, his great epic poem in the spirit of Homer, Augustus immediately placed it on the curriculum for Roman school children. He paid a similar tribute to *Vitruvius*, a lesser known writer, for his De Architectura, a summary of known techniques in building construction, military devices and visual perspective.

Reflection: This era is still a controversial one as it appears different depending on whether one supports the Senate and the Republic, or Caesar, Mark Antony and Octavian. As with the civil (Peloponnesian) war among Greeks, the Roman Civil War and early Empire coincided with a colossal cultural outburst. This Golden Era both preserved and embellished our cultural heritage.

Crossing the Rubicon.

Iconic Event: Caesar crossing the Rubicon does capture the spirit of the Age. It reflects the dilemma that the intransigent Senate had imposed upon its military leaders. The only protection for such leaders was to be named "dictator for life" while they controlled of the Army. After Julius was killed, his nephew addressed the problem and gave Rome 45 years of stability!

Chapter 10: GOLDEN AGE OF ROMAN CULTURE, 60 BCE to 18 CE.

The Golden Age of Roman Culture begins with Cicero in 60 BCE. As Mary Beard points out, the writings of Cicero are a dramatic change from the past in that they survived, they are numerous, and are of a very high quality. His surviving works include about 60 orations, 15 or so philosophical essays (in the style of Aristotle and Plato), and over 900 letters to friends and public figures, such as Crassus, Pompey and Caesar. He wrote in Latin, but was well versed in Greek thought, especially relating to rhetoric. His Greek slave, Tiro, was his scribe and, even after his death, devotedly collected and preserved his writings.

But, Cicero was not the only great classic writer of this Era: several other Romans proudly demonstrated their ability to both synthesize and build on Greek thinking and techniques in rhetoric, history, literature, philosophy, sculpture, architecture, astronomy and medicine.

Rhetoric: *Cicero*, 114 to 43 BCE, persuasively advocated for the importance of rhetoric, the art of verbal persuasion, as a field of study for all youth. He was a Roman senator, a general, and was once elected consul; his contemporaries sought him out when they required an advocate. Two of his essays elaborate on the role and techniques of successful orators and orations. Also, the 60 or so of his surviving speeches show he had learned, respected, applied, and embellished Greek rhetorical principles. Generations later, *Quintilian* (35 to 100 CE), an admirer of the writings of Cicero, added further to our understanding of rhetoric, with his seminal work, Institutio Oratoria, that summarized both Greek and Roman thought on the subject.

History: *Cicero* also marked a breakthrough for historians! His 900 letters to others are an unprecedented window into the events of his lifetime and a primary source for those seeking to learn about the private concerns of a wealthy Roman. There was no similar trove of missives from any earlier time. A second landmark was *Julius Caesar's* Commentaries on the Gallic Wars. It is a wonderfully written, crisp and clear, memoir, and became a standard text for Latin students, even into the 20th century. Only *Ulysses S. Grant*'s Memoir is held in equally high esteem as a military autobiography.

Additionally, the Era produced several other excellent historians that either witnessed current events or credited the reports of earlier Greek and Roman histories that are no longer available to us. (*See Appendix #5 for more on Historians*).

Literature: Roman literature followed Greek example, using verse and rhyme to facilitate both oral performance and memorization (as few copies were available). While modern writers praise both Caesar and Cicero for their prose literary excellence, ancient audiences prized their poets.

Virgil (70-19 BCE) was already an established and famous poet when The Aeneid was published just after his death. Indeed, his tale of the founding of Rome and the odyssey of his hero Aeneas from Troy to Carthage to Rome was so compelling for Romans, Augustus made it required reading in Roman schools. His Georgics, (29 BCE) is also notable: it is a call for peace masquerading as as a field manual for Roman farmers.

Horace (65 BCE to 8 CE) was another favorite of Augustus. He steadily demonstrated excellence with Epodes (29 BCE) and Centennial Hymn (17 BCE). His masterpiece though was Odes (23-24 BCE); a series of short poems that stress alliteration and skilled wordplay rather than epic storytelling.

Ovid (43 BCE to16 CE) never benefited from imperial support. Augustus promoted sexual austerity and Ovid's early masterpieces were Amores (20 BCE) and The Art of Love (1 BCE). The latter was a tongue in cheek manual of the stratagems each gender employs to entice the other. Ovid's masterpiece though, is Metamorphoses (8 BCE), which dips into Greek mythology to tell 250 themed short stories about changes from human to animal to plant.

Philosophy: Cicero's philosophical writings reflect the continued interest among educated Romans in Aristotle and Plato in that his many dialogues imitated their style. Nearly as subtle, *Militius'* De Astronomica is a thoughtful poem that both summarizes Roman understanding of astronomy and relates it to Greek Stoic thinking.

Even so, *Lucretius'* (95-55 BCE) De Rerum Natura, (*On the Nature of Things*), is the Masterpiece of the Era. It is an amazing poem that ties together the atomic theory of Democritus and the ideas of the Greek philosopher Epicurus.

Sculpture and Architecture: On his deathbed, Augustus famously claimed that he turned Rome from a city of brick into one of marble. Sculpture also shifted from bronze to marble. Much of the new construction and design was made possible as Romans gradually discovered that cement made with lime and volcanic ash was stronger. Augustus authorized construction for many new public facilities. Maybe the most important of these is the Pantheon.

Pantheon: the first version of the Pantheon was likely begun during the consulship of Augustus's friend, Marcus Agrippa, and built between 29-19 BCE. It began as a Temple of Mars, and scholars still argue whether its dome was original, came after the fire of 80 CE, or when Trajan rebuilt it in 114 CE. Almost 2000 years after construction, this dome is still a marvel, the largest in the world made with unreinforced concrete. The height and diameter are the same: 142 feet.

The other significant achievement in architecture was *Vitruvius'* De Architectura. This striking book is a manual describing what Greeks and Romans had learned about architecture. This included detailed information about constructing aqueducts, libraries, temples and other public buildings, as well as artillery, hoists, and, from the Greeks, the importance of perspective in building design. To illustrate the importance of perspective, he employed a drawing of a man, called the Vitruvian man.

Medicine: *Aulus Cornelius Celsus,* 23-50 BCE, is another example of the Roman penchant for synthesizing the knowledge of both Greek and Roman thinkers on a given topic. Celsus was an encyclopedist who wrote several such tomes; but only De Medicina has survived. In it, he emphasizes the importance of cleanliness and provides details about recommended doses of medicines. Much of what we know about Hellenistic medicine comes from this book. It revealed to medieval society just how advanced Rome medicine had been in comparison.

Galen, 129-216 BCE, was Greek and grew up in Pergamum. He took a more empirical approach to medicine, and his work, at least in the East, would come to supersede Celsus. He learned about the human body by working on wounded gladiators and, while in Alexandria, dissecting monkeys in order to better understand the human circulation and nerve systems. About 20,000 pages of his works survive.

Initially, he had more influence in the Eastern Mediterranean, and this heightened after 850 CE when 129 of his works were translated into Arabic and Syrian.

Astronomy: With the above-mentioned exception of Miletius's poem that meshes philosophy and astronomy, Rome's Golden Age, relied on the ideas and research from Alexandria. The dominant astronomer for the next 1400 years though was Ptolemy. His <u>Almagest</u> written about 150 CE described an earth-centered and mathematical concept of the universe for astronomical forecasts.

The most singular astronomical achievement of this Golden Age, the adoption of the Julian calendar, came as a suggestion from Alexandria's leading astronomer *Sosigenes of Alexandria* who is also credited with accurately describing the orbit of Mercury. As *Pliny the Elder* tells the story, Caesar met Sosigenes while visiting Cleopatra (47-46 BCE). Sosigenes suggested a system proposed centuries earlier by *Aristarchus of Samos*: a 12 month, 365 day year with an extra day added every four years. Caesar, with help from Sosigenes, then implemented this in 46 BCE shortly after he became Dictator. It quickly became the standard for the next 1600 years until Pope Gregory XIII modified it slightly in 1583.

Reflection: Many of the writers of this period mark the peak of Greco-Roman understanding of our cultural heritage in both the arts and sciences. Some were encyclopedists who organized and passed on this collective body of knowledge. Notably, most of the scientific and mathematical advances come from the East where the Greek language prevailed. Perhaps, Roman numerals were too awkward for such purposes.

This body of learning had already dodged several bullets: conquest by Macedonia, again by Rome, and several civil wars. It is fortunate that Alexander and Augustus were educated persons who loved this culture. When the Wheel of Fortune finally turned against Rome, though, what would happen to this body of learning they so carefully protected?

Iconic Event: The iconic events of the Era are the projects favored by Augustus. He supported the poetic works' of Virgil and Horace, but not the more 'salacious' Ovid. He loved construction projects as well, and promoted Vitruvius's famous "how to" handbook, De Architectura. Perhaps the most famed project that he supported was the Pantheon.

Chapter 11: CULTURAL TRANSITION, 100-600 CE.

It is during this era that large stumbling blocks force major detours along the Twisty Trail from here to Copernicus. It is a complex and tumultuous time, so let's consider it in three phases: from 100-300 CE; the Age from Constantine to Theodosius; the Rise of Christian Culture.

The Empire from 100-300 CE:

By and large this is a stable period. From a territorial perspective, the Empire confronted continuous threats from the north and east just to maintain its power, which it mostly did.

Politically, the style of government gradually morphed from hereditary absolute monarchy to army control. Successorship was a lingering problem. Once the Army took over the institutions of the empire, assassination became the most common method of imperial successorship. In the 50 years from 235 to 284, there were over 30 emperors: all but one died violently. The Emperor Diocletian (284-306) recognized the problem, often called the *Crisis of the Third Century*. Accordingly, in 286, he appointed another "Augustus" to rule the West while retaining the wealthier East for himself. Seven years later, he named subordinate leaders, called "Caesar", for each "Augustus". His notion was that each officer would move up in an orderly fashion in the event of his anyone's demise.

Culturally, Emperors and citizens added significant landmarks to their legacy. The already mentioned contributions of *Galen* and *Dioscorides* in Medicine and *Ptolemy* in Science and Astronomy, for example, actually belong to this period. Those treatises, as we will see, are among the 10 or so most sought after in future centuries. Trajan's rebuilt and domed Pantheon of 117 is another impressive feat. We can see it now! At about the same time, Trajan also built Rome's Forum that included two libraries: one for Greek and the other for Latin writings. Scholars think they had up to 20,000 scrolls.

One cultural issue was becoming worrisome: religion. While Roman leaders of the Augustan Age and earlier were comfortable with Greek culture, the interaction between Greco-Roman and Jewish and Christian cultures was more complex and sometimes led to riots. As Bart Ehrman points out in his Triumph of Christianity, (2018), Roman religion was cultic and inclusive. Like the Greeks and Persians before them, they were tolerant and did not require conversion to their specific form of worship. Among pagans, the cultic practices were familiar: there were animal sacrifices, prayers for continued protection from wars and storms, and a reading of animal entrails to divine the future. Indeed, Romans often adopted as their own the more appealing gods of their conquered peoples. The important thing was that worship occur to retain the good grace of the gods.

Things were more complicated with the Jewish sect, which made up about 5% of the Empire in 325. Similarities included practicing prayer and animal sacrifice. While

Jews would not worship other gods, they tolerated those who did. Uniquely, they made their sacrifices specifically to compensate for their sins rather than as a generic way to please their god. (see Leviticus and Deuteronomy). The Jewish God was offended by sin, while others were indifferent.

Ehrman reports that the consensus of scholars is that the Christian sect was about 7% of the Empire in 300. This is after the Diocletian persecution! Their leader, Jesus, died about 30 CE. He had advocated "rendering to Caesar what was Caesar's" and "turning the other cheek". Yet, he also taught that earthly kingdoms were unimportant: there was an afterlife where righteous persons would be citizens of a much better Kingdom of Heaven.

Romans sometimes sensed treason in this claim of a higher loyalty! Like Jews, Christians would not worship other gods. Emperors occasionally authorized persecutions, but these often backfired, as everyday Romans increasingly came to respect the commitment and bravery of the martyrs.

The New Testament is the earliest example of Christian literature. Christians wrote in Greek, the universal language understood throughout the Empire. They travelled on newly created or improved Roman roads. Enough were educated so that, by 54 CE, they were sharing letters of encouragement among their growing communities including: Antioch, Jerusalem, Corinth, Philippi, Ephesus and Rome. By 100 CE, several witnesses recorded their own testimonies concerning their experience of the wisdom and teachings of Jesus. Papyrus versions of these currently exist, dated about 200-250 CE. The New Testament is marvelous literature composed, like the Old Testament, by several different authors. This adds to its sense of authenticity!

Jesus taught in parables to convey his message that the spiritual world was more important than the empirical one. The Apostle Paul also expressed this vividly in First Corinthians: "all knowledge will pass away...now we see as through a glass darkly; then face to face. Now I know in part, then, I will know fully"! Similarly, Plato's **Republic** compares the human ability to perceive to that of slaves chained inside a cave such that they can only see shadows on a wall but not what is causing the figures to be there. These slaves, though, come to think that the shadows are the entirety of reality. This Platonist philosophical position of early Christian thinkers will rock the Twisty Trail.

From Constantine to Theodosius:

The reign of *Constantine the Great,* 306-337 CE, is when the cultural and political paths of the Eastern and Western Empire diverge. To my mind, Constantine took three actions that, over the long term, resulted in a dimming of Rome's cultural brilliance over the next seven centuries: (1) he moved the capital from Rome to Constantinople: (2) he collected the scrolls needed for establishing the Great Library of Constantinople he planned; (3) he tolerated and supported Christianity. This latter, among other consequences, led Jerome in 382 to begin translating the Old and New Testament into Latin. He completed this in

405. An unintended result was to further isolate the Roman/Latin world from achievements in Greek or other languages.

Moving the Capital: Constantine decided to move the capital eastward for very practical reasons:
1. Constantinople was easier to defend, nearly impregnable;
2. It is located at the nexus of Europe and Asia as well as the Mediterranean and the Black seas;
3. It was closer than Rome to the wealthier parts of the Empire such as Asia Minor, Egypt and Mesopotamia.
4. It was at the crucial location at the center of where legions located throughout the Empire.

One immediate result was Rome's loss of many educated citizens and artisans who soon moved East to be near the new center of government. This move also made Rome more vulnerable to invasions such as occurred in 410. Population estimates for Rome (based on food shipments) show some of the impact: Rome's 5 BCE population was at least 800,000; in 419 CE, it had fallen to 400,000. It gets worse! In 430, the Vandals shut off grain supplies to the city; then barbarians sacked it in both 455 and 476. The estimates for 590 are 150,000. By 800 CE, only 30,000!

This is a lot to place at Constantine's feet. Other unforeseeable and contributory major events had nothing to do with him! These include the rise of the Greek speaking Byzantine Empire and of Arabic Islam. The effect of both of these events was to isolate the Latin West from the rest of Mediterranean culture.

Equally significant, Paul Freedman, in his online Yale lecture, "The Transformation of Rome", notes that the new 'barbarian" kings just didn't have the economic resources to feed such a great city. Most were without navies and so could not control, or even influence, Mediterranean trade routes. In short, they could not maintain Rome in its standard of living. Some scholars have described this era after 410 as a "Dark Age". Others merely portray it as a dimmer age. Either way, there was a gradual but dramatic drop in both its quality of life and its receptiveness to the ideas of the Ancient past.

Great Library of Constantinople: Constantine, a Latin speaker, initiated a program to transcribe Greek and some Latin masterpieces from papyrus onto longer lasting parchment. His son Constantius took the next step, in 357 CE, of actually building a new library. He charged it with both preservation of documents and their transfer to parchment. The Emperor Valens, in 372, continued this governmental support by providing four Greek and 3 Latin calligraphers for the project. We know the library prioritized ancient Greek works, and held over 100,000 texts: many were copies from the Alexandria Library. While Rome had once boasted some 28 libraries, after the Fall in 456, they had nothing to compare with Constantinople. Most of the Constantinople texts were in Greek: Latin-speaking West Europeans could no longer read them!

Tolerating and Supporting Christianity:

Christians were only 7% of the Empire's population in 300 CE, but would be about 50% just a hundred years later. Bart Ehrman summarizes several of the reasons that experts offer for this success. Three of these resonate with me as compelling:

1. <u>A Miraculous work of God</u>. Certainly, as Ehrman notes, most converts gave miracles as their primary reason for converting.
2. <u>A Consistent rate of Growth</u>. While growth from 5 MM to 30 MM in 100 years seems impressive, Ehrman notes it is only the steady projection of previous compounded rates of 2.5% per year.
3. <u>State Protection and Support</u>. Pagan aristocrats and government leaders were the basis of financial support for temples and statues and celebrations. As these converted to Christianity, so did their support for pagan culture.

<u>Miracles</u>: Constantine and many of his officers believed his 312 CE victory in the Battle of Milvian Bridge was a miracle. He converted as he promised. This set a marker for those who wanted his trust. After 313, his religion was no longer subject to persecution. On the contrary, Constantine became a steady supporter of various Christian projects such as new church construction. To illustrate, in 324, Constantine began destroying pagan temples in his new city so he could provide it with an overtly Christian architecture. A vivid example is his decision to demolish the Temple to Aphrodite and replace

it with a new Christian cathedral on that site. He dedicated his new city in 330.

Over the next 60 years, all but one of the subsequent emperors were Christian. They frowned more and more on pagan cults. Finally, in 391, the Emperor Theodosius, 379-95, made Christianity (and Judaism) the only legal religions of the Empire.

<u>A Consistent Rate of Growth:</u> In his appendix to <u>Triumph of Christianity,</u> Ehrman analyzes the available numbers to show that the annually growth rate of 2.5% is not an unreasonable one in light of what know of its prior growth.

<u>State Protection and Support</u>: In ancient days, religion and state were inextricable. Once there was a steady stream of Christian emperors, a flood of local and provincial magistrates and aristocrats would gradually transfer their allegiances and funding to the support of Christian projects, and pagan ones would wither.

All three factors played important roles, but my sense is that #3 was decisive. Regardless of the specific cause, a dramatic shift began during this era. For the previous 1000 plus years, 95% of the Mediterranean peoples practiced cultic animal sacrifice, worshipped many gods, built temples and sculptures to honor their gods, and tolerated other faiths. Christians, by contrast, worshipped one God only. Uniquely, He wanted people to turn from sin rather than make animal sacrifices. The great pagan statues and temples were anathema and an affront to their jealous God.

Rise of a Christian Culture:

Early Christian writings reflected the writings of Saint Paul and challenged the Aristotelian assumption that the world was knowable through science and reason. Like Plato, they contended that the spiritual world is more real, if less knowable. This Platonic streak is a major aspect of our Classic Heritage, but one that, as it actually developed, led Europe to a murky future. Here are the works of some of the major Christian thinkers:

Confessions: *Augustine of Hippo*, 354-430 CE, was a well-educated person and on the fast track marked for success in the Roman Empire. He was well read in both Plato and Aristotle. He wrote over a hundred books, but this one, written between 397 and 400, is the first known instance of a spiritual memoir by anyone in the West. His moment of conversion comes when he discovers that reason and education are not needed for salvation. Rather, there must be an emotional and heartfelt commitment to faith in God. This book, and his second, <u>City of God</u>, were the two most influential throughout the Christian Middle Ages.

The Consolation of Philosophy: *Boethius*, 477-524 CE, was another writer important to the Middle Ages. He was an ambassador to Constantinople and a well-read scholar, influenced by both Plato and Aristotle. He had translated many minor Greek works into Latin. His <u>Consolation</u> was written while he was in jail awaiting execution for treason. The book is a dialogue covering many philosophical topics, including death and fortune. He likens life and fate to a turning of the Wheel of Fortune with consolation being found only in the spiritual life beyond this one. His subsequent death itself turned the Wheel of Fortune against a quicker cultural invigoration for Europeans. It prevented him from starting his next project: translating all of Plato and Aristotle from Greek to Latin: a project that few of his contemporaries had the skill to do.

Benedictine Monasteries: *Benedict of Nursia*, 480-547, founded 12 monasteries in his lifetime. His <u>Rule of Saint Benedict</u> guided the abbeys of his own order, but also influenced many of the other new orders that would follow. These rules emphasized the importance of prayer, work, and study. The latter, important to our essay, often included making copies of old manuscripts, religious and otherwise. His followers founded four Benedictine monasteries devoted to transcribing and famous for their libraries: Reichenau (724); Fulda (744); Saint Gallen (747); and Cluny (910). Without their work, much classic knowledge would have never been found.

Etymologies (*aka* Origines): For the few Christians who could read, this book was their academic text throughout the middle and late middle ages. *Isidore of Seville*, 560-636, was a bishop and scholar. This text, published 600-625, was an encyclopedia of knowledge that stitched together Latin translations of select and approved excerpts of Greek texts relevant to a given topic. Some of the texts we currently have are passed on to us only in this book. Many of the portions omitted are still lost. <u>Origines</u> was popular well into the Renaissance and boasted 10 printed editions between 1472 and 1530.

Reflection: *Edward Gibbon*, in the History of the Decline and Fall of the Roman Empire, 1778, attributed this decline to the rise of Christianity. To me, the wise and strategic decision to relocate the capital of the Empire to Constantinople was the turning point. It isolated the city from Greek Culture, reduced its educated classes, and made the city more vulnerable to invasion.

The question of why Christianity spread is intertwined. I believe Constantine converted because of the Miracle at the Milvian Bridge. Pagan kings often attributed their victories to their gods (Darius the Great comes to mind) and established temples in their honor (Athena and Athens). Constantine's actions are similar. A difference is that as subsequent Christians won victories, credit went to the same One God and gradually crowded out the others. Further, pagan temples and festivals depended upon financial support from local magistrates. Once leaders became Christian, their faith forbade them from also funding pagan temples.

Iconic Event: Saint Jerome's authorship of the Vulgate, the Latin translation from the Hebrew Old Testament and the Greek New Testament, in 405, had an incredibly long shelf-life. It was faithfully and reliably re-copied throughout the Middle Ages, and was among the first books printed after the invention of the printing press in the1450s. Secondly, I note that Jerome did much of his work in Bethlehem, Judea, near where most of the described events took place. This likely improved his work due to the proximity of Jewish scholars to consult with. While his Latin version of the Christian Bible greatly facilitated outreach to Western Europe, it also make the

West more isolated from any cultural breakthroughs by Greek-speakers in the East.

SAINT JEROME IN HIS STUDY:

Chapter 12: THE ISLAMIC YEARS, 600-1031 CE.

By 600 CE, prospects were bleak for preserving, let alone enhancing, Greco-Roman culture. One factor was the devastating Fall of Rome to barbarians. Equally fatal was Christian suspicion and hostility to pagan artifacts, temples and writings.

Suddenly, a barely noticed character actor came onto the stage from out of an Eastern desert. He took the lead role, and, in still another plot twist, took key steps that inadvertently salvaged much of this heritage.

Spread of Islam: Little is known about pre-Islamic Arabic: there are only five extant inscriptions. The oldest instance of an Arabic inscription dates to 352 CE; it is a consonant-based offshoot of Aramaic. By 900, though, it supplanted Greek and become the primary language used in the Mediterranean for scientific inquiry.

Mohammed, himself, was born in 570 (please assume CE hereafter unless otherwise noted), had his Revelation from the Angel Gabriel when he was forty, and unified Arabs behind the Muslim faith by 632. Then, he died without a son. A struggle promptly ensued between family members and those who were part of his inner military circle, over who should lead the movement. By 661, the Umayyads, an inner-circle family from Mecca, emerged from the pack, assumed leadership, and unified all Muslims until 750.

Along the way, Umayyad forces battled those who favored a hereditary leadership. In 680, they decisively defeated them and beheaded Muhammad's grandson, igniting a 1500-year bitter split between Sunnis and Shiites that still festers today. Under Umayyad caliphs (caliph means successor), Islam spread swiftly. They occupied Egypt (642); conquered Persia (651) including parts of India; and absorbed North Africa and Visigothic Spain (712). Islam finally peaked by unsuccessfully besieging Constantinople in 717 and a losing a battle with Christians in 733 near Poitiers, France. At its zenith, it was the largest contiguous Empire ever, and included 5 million square miles.

ISLAMIC EMPIRE:

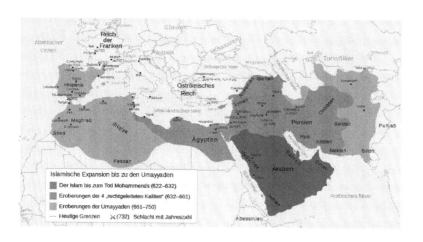

Scholars marvel at the speedy spread of both the Empire and the Faith. Like the Persians, Romans, and Greeks before them, they did not require the conquered to convert.

They let them keep their faith, their businesses, and their land, charging the unconverted a tax. Even so conversions did follow. (The intolerance sometimes associated with some Muslims came much later).

The Abbasids and the House of Wisdom: Despite these successes, the grumbling against the Umayyads increased after they lost some key battles, and once others noticed that non-Arabs, a growing portion of Muslims, were seldom appointed to leadership positions. Supporters of the Abbasids, many of them Persians, had a far more inclusive vision of the Muslim future. Even so, after the Abbasids took power in 750, they invited the Umayyads to a Reconciliation Banquet, and massacred all of those who attended.

The Abbasids focused on culturally uniting, rather than expanding, the empire. One of the earliest steps they took, in 756, was to move the capital from Damascus (near the Mediterranean) to Baghdad (nearer to Persia and India). By 800, the recently constructed new city of Baghdad, with over a million people, was the largest and wealthiest city in the world! A century later, the tally was 2 million!

As a next step, the caliph constructed, in 830, a **House of Wisdom** where the learning of India, China, Persia, Arabia and especially Greece intermingled. The goal was to translate everything into Arabic, the new language of diplomacy in the East, and to conduct research that helped the Muslim faithful. Such work began soon after 771 when a delegation of Indian scholars, bringing texts, visited Baghdad.

A third significant development was that the Abbasids learned from the Chinese how to make **paper**. Baghdad then built in 793 a factory of its own and this dramatically reduced the cost of writing for official records, business, and scholarly purposes. By 1100, the caliphate had several such factories: including one in 1056 in Javita, Spain. The rest of western Europe had none.

The intercultural collaboration is well illustrated in **Mathematics.** It begins with Greek geometry and the early translation into Arabic of *Euclid's* <u>Elements</u>. Then, *Al Khwarizmi,* 780-850, a Persian scholar, who was Director of the House of Wisdom wrote a book, in Arabic, that promoted the Hindu numbering system, which uses a zero and nine other integers, as the most flexible and precise. Beyond addition and subtraction, this system permits decimals, and thus, enables more accurate calculations. He was the first to determine the first 16 digits of *pi*.

Al Khwarizmi pushed this concept further in a book of his own that explains the importance of decimals and invents Algebra (he is the "Father of Algebra"), including quadratic equations. Similarly, having learned from the Hindu mathematicians about the trigonometric value of the sine function, he pushed on to invent the cosine, tangent, cotangent, secant, and cosecant. All were needed to calculate the movements of the sun, moon, stars and planets.

Meanwhile, the Latin West was struggling to add or subtract numbers using a Roman numeral system!

Medicine was another Greek specialty, so Greek translation to Arabic was the principle method here of cultural diffusion. *Dioscorides* was a Greek physician who served in the Roman Army between 50-70 CE. His De Materia Medicina, a pharmacology, came from the Byzantines in about 950 CE. Once translated, it became the standard Arabic hospital text. Second, while none of *Galen of Pergamum's* (129-216) work had been translated into Latin before 1000, he was the major resource in Byzantine medical thinking. Once House of Wisdom scholars obtained copies, they translated 129 of his treatises from Greek to Arabic.

Astronomy: *Al-Khwarizmi* also focused on astronomy. Muslim leaders saw astronomy as a way to show the value of their research to more conservative Muslims. Algebra, trigonometry, decimals and quadratic equations were all important to the Caliph since they were needed to accurately establish the times for the five daily prayers in hundreds of locations throughout the empire. Similar, but more exacting, calculations were required to predict crescent moons and lunar months. Also, the ability to predict equinoxes and eclipses was a critical skill that impressed pagans.

Philosophy: Islamic leaders were convinced that science and religion were part of the same knowledge system. *Al*

Kindi (801-873), a Syrian, was another leader at the House of Wisdom. He collected many Greek manuscripts, mostly from Byzantium, and supervised their translation from Greek to Arabic. These included not only *Dioscorides* and *Galen* (Medicine), *Euclid* (Mathematics), Plato and Aristotle (Philosophy), but also the jewel of the intellectual crown: Ptolemy's <u>Almagest</u>. This was the starting point for a comprehensive theory about the motion of planets, stars, the moon and sun.

Al Kindi also had a strong interest in the translations of Aristotle and Plato. His own masterpiece, <u>Treatise on Intellect</u>, aimed to reconcile Islam with the philosophical works of Plato and especially Aristotle. He emphasized the latter's proof of God, the prime mover, as the starting point. Islamic and Christian objections to Aristotle were a primary obstacle to their embrace of classic culture.

For Arabs, translation was merely a starting point for their study. They wrote and published annotations on what they read, noted new supporting or contrary data, and composed separate commentaries to clarify the intent of what they read.

Decline: After 150 years, Boethius's Wheel of Fortune slowly turned against the Abbasids. After 909 CE, they gradually became figureheads rather than rulers. Soon the emirs in Persia, Egypt and Cordoba declared independent caliphates of their own. The Dynasty ended in 1258 when splendid and wealthy Baghdad fell to the Mongols who destroyed everything, including the paper books and scrolls in the House of Wisdom. One observer noted that the Tigris River turned black from all the ink.

Cordoba, Spain: The one Umayyad prince who shrewdly decided not to attend the Reconciliation Banquet of 750 CE journeyed instead from North Africa to Cordoba, Spain. There, in 756, the population acclaimed him as emir. He declared his loyalty to the caliphate 3000 miles away, and they left him alone.

A Second Umayyad Dynasty thus started in Spain in 756. Its leaders emulated Baghdad in cultural effort and achievement. By 950, Cordoba would have 90,000 people, the largest city in Europe: the second largest, also in Spain, was Zaragoza with 28,000. The prize jewel among its architectural achievements is "The Great Mosque of Cordoba", (785-791), famed for its "horseshoe arches", and one of the "Wonders of the World". It is still standing, as is the impressive Fortress at Malaga. The Umayyad palace in Cordoba was the most splendid one in Europe!

Like the early Abbasids, the Spanish Umayyads were firmly committed to learning. Cordoba boasted 70 libraries with over 400,000 manuscripts, mainly using **paper.** Over the years from 850 to 1085, they obtained copies, through the Abbasids, of Arabic masterworks such as those by Al Kindi and Al-Khwarizmi. They modified Al-Khwarizmi's "star tables", changing the times and motions of stars over Baghdad to ones that reflected readings from Cordoba. From Baghdad, they obtained Arabic translations of many key Greek texts such as Euclid's Elements, Aristotle's

Physics; and Ptolemy's Almagest. Dissatisfied with the quality of the extant Arabic version of Dioscorides De Materia Medica, they established a multicultural team of medical scholars to do a better one. This collaboration would be a model for the future.

Gerbert of Aurillac (961-1003) was born in Barcelona and studied in Seville and Cordoba where he learned Arabic mathematics. In 980, he wrote a four page tract in Latin that explained to his readers a "new math" that used the Hindu numbering system (nine digits and a dot, instead of a "0"). To some, it was an obvious improvement; to others, it reeked of Muslim witchcraft and magic. He was often accused of sorcery because he could calculate so much faster than those who used Roman numbers. The new system caught on slowly, even though, when Gerbert became Pope Sylvester II in 999, he did all he could to promote it during his short reign before his death in 1003.

It would be three more centuries before Europeans would abandon their Roman numerals.

Reflection: Dear reader, I was so surprised to just now learn that Persia, India, China and the Arabs had added so much during this era to our Greco-Roman Cultural Heritage. I was also very impressed how committed Arabs were to adopting Greek, Persian and Indian ideas, and how willing they were to learn from others. In preserving and expanding their own collective knowledge, they set the table, as we will see, for western thinkers many centuries later.

Meanwhile, the amazing life story of Gerbert and his efforts to promote the 'new math' reminds me that "you can bring a horse to water, but you can't make him drink". In 771, the Arabs were ready for better addition and subtraction, but also decimals, quadratic equations, pi, and trigonometry. Regrettably, Europeans outside of Spain, in 999, were even afraid to start the voyage.

Iconic Event: Surely the event that best captures the Spirit of the Age is the visit in 771 of the Hindu delegation to Bagdad. It was an unexpected and amazing instance of technology transfer. They brought "star tables" reflecting readings from Aram, a city in India.

The House of Wisdom went on to compose "star tables" for what they could see from Baghdad. The scholars of India also brought the concepts of zero, decimals, and the beginnings of trigonometry.

The Twisty Trail

Chapter 13: THE AGE OF REDISCOVERY, 1000-1400 CE

In God's Crucible, *David Levering Lewis* identifies 1002 as the year Muslim Spain reached its military pinnacle. Its greatest general, *Al Mansur*, 976-1002, had totally humiliated the Christian nations in northern Spain, razing their sacred shrine of Santiago de Compostela in 997. The site was the terminus of a major pilgrimage trail for thousands every year. Al Mansur had won 50 consecutive battles, enslaved many Christians, and carried off the Bells from the Cathedral at Compostela.

However, over the next 30 years, the Wheel of Fortune tipped again and the Spanish Caliphate grew gradually weaker until, in 1031, it finally dissolved into a series of petty kingdoms, each with its own palace, library, and the like. Meanwhile, the Christian kings united and began a *Reconquista* of Spain. There were many battles back and forth. But the one that matters most for our story of Classical heritage happened in 1085 when a Christian army surprised Muslim forces and captured Toledo and its fabulous library.

Similarly, just 10 years later, Pope Urban II called for a Crusade that led to many colorful characters, grisly battles, and cruel and bloody massacres. The important matter here, though, is that Crusaders captured Antioch, once the second largest city in the East, and its famous library in June of 1098.

These two events, ten years apart, set in motion a twisty series of events that led the West to rediscover its cultural roots and, in turn, initiate its Renaissance.

Antioch, 1114-1126: Abelard of Bath, 1080-1152, was an English cleric and scholar who traveled to France, Italy and Sicily. Likely, he learned Arabic while in the Muslim city of Syracuse in Sicily. He had an unquenchable thirst for knowledge, and quickly grew very dissatisfied with what Europe had to offer, especially in Mathematics, as compared with what Arabs already knew. He authored three influential books, including one modelled on Boethius's <u>Consolation of Philosophy.</u> Aware that Antioch, one of the region's largest cities, had a large library and that Crusaders still controlled the region, he took himself, and his working knowledge of Arabic, to Antioch sometime before the great earthquake there in 1114.

Abelard spent at least 12 years there and discovered and translated Euclid's masterpiece, <u>Elements of Geometry</u>, from Arabic into Latin. In his own lifetime, this brought him fame and a reputation as a scholar. Interest was so strong that *Campanus of Navarro*, using Abelard's translation from the Arabic as well as his own Greek version, published a new Latin translation of <u>Elements</u> in the mid-13th century. This was printed in 1482, and became the standard version of Euclid for centuries. Geometry was the first form of mathematics readily accepted in scholarly Europe.

His second achievement was translating Al-Khwarizmi's Star Tables into Latin. In that process, he learned the Arabic numeral system. Realizing its significance, and the underlying math needed to grasp it, he wrote a pamphlet introducing and explaining the value and workings of the "new" Arabic-Hindu number and computation system (still with no zero). Regrettably, his work did not catch on for another century. This occurred after 1202 when *Fibonacci*, a mathematical genius, produced Liber Abaci. This work introduces the zero, and patiently explains the value of the Arabic number system for trade, record keeping and commerce. It was so successful that there was a second printing in 1228.

Other scholars also searched the Antioch library while that was possible, but their finds were not among the more influential texts we have been tracking.

Toledo, 1130-80: While Christians captured Toledo in 1085, it was not until 1130 that its new king called together a group of Jewish, Islamic, and Christian scholars to collaborate in translating its Greek and Arabic texts into Latin.

Their leading scholar, *Gerard of Cremona,* 1114-1187, a Christian cleric, completed over 70 translations from Arabic or Greek to Latin. Some of his more important manuscripts include:

Archimedes, On the Measurement of the Circle
Aristotle, On the Heavens: Physics
Galen, (various medical topics)

Ptolemy, <u>Almagest</u> (translated in 1175)
Al Khwarizmi, <u>On Algebra</u>
Al Kindi, <u>De Intellectu</u>

Two other more contemporary Arabic manuscripts also reached Europe via Toledo. One was Avicenna's, 980-1037, <u>Canon of Medicine</u> which summarized all Arabic medical knowledge. It eventually became the primary medical text of Europe.

The second was more controversial: <u>Commentaries</u> by *Averroes,* 1126-98, a native of Cordoba. His work was a commentary and translation of Aristotle that convincingly contends that Aristotle and Religion are compatible with one another. *Thomas Aquinas,* 1225-74, the leading Christian philosopher of the late Middle Ages, often and respectfully called him "the Commentator". Like Al-Kindi and Aquinas, Averroes encountered opposition from many leading Christians. They noted that while Reason could prove a God existed; it could not prove the existence of one who is personal or currently active. They believed Faith was the only reliable path to God.

Reflection #1: Nearly all of these early discoveries and translations focused on mathematical, scientific or philosophical works. Except for Euclid, these were sometimes suspiciously received! Sadly, Latin Europeans were just not ready for Hindu numbers, but, without them, they could not begin to grasp Algebra or Trigonometry--or even decimals. This is several centuries away.

There is no record of translations done of major Greek or Roman writings in Rhetoric or Literature.

The University of Paris, 1215-1272, during this period, was widely recognized as the premier European institution for teaching theology or philosophy. As such, it was ground zero for the battle over Aristotle.

We know that Europe's first exposure to Aristotle was through Averroes' <u>Commentaries</u>. There must also have been copies available of Aristotle's Physics and his Metaphysics before 1215 as the University banned them in that year. Interest in the Great Philosopher likely continued as they had to ban them again in 1231.

Tensions inflamed as *Siger of Brant,* 1240-1281, a professor of philosophy at Paris, heavily influenced by Averroes and Aristotle, taught in 1260 that, while the soul was immortal, after death it merged into a single Great soul. Since this was not mentioned in either the Old or New Testaments, traditionalists were outraged.

In 1268, *Thomas Aquinas,* 1225-1274, was sent back to Paris to deal with this crisis. His writings took ideas from both Averroists, such as Siger, and from the traditionalists in the Church. Aristotle and the Averroists had argued that reason alone sufficed to show there was a Prime Mover or First Cause. Christian, Jewish and Muslim opponents, as noted earlier, grumbled that this was a deist conception that left no room for an active and responsive God. In Summa Theologica, Thomas promoted a "middle way" that expanded the role of reason while emphasizing the importance of Faith. In doing so, he steered the ship of Christian thought just a bit more toward Reason, Science, and Aristotle. And, also, a bit further away from the reliance on Faith that characterized past centuries. As a result, Aristotle became more widely accepted!

Aquinas's views were not universally embraced! To address the suspicion of traditionalists against perceived Arab heresies, he used Latin translations directly from the

Greek that *William of Moerbeke* produced between 1260-71. Moerbeke was an established expert in translating Greek into Latin who also did a Latin translation from the Greek of *Archimedes* <u>On the Measurement of the Circle.</u>

Northern Italy, 1333-1427, was the birthplace of the Renaissance. Historians credit *Petrarch 1304-74*, by consensus the greatest scholar of the Age, with initiating the Rebirth of Classical Culture into Europe that we call the Renaissance. He did this, most say, in 1333 when he found two of Cicero's <u>Orations</u> while visiting a local monastery. He continued stirring enthusiasm for the Classics when he published a series of letters he wrote to long dead scholars, Cicero and Virgil. Inspired further when he visited the ruins of classical Rome in 1337, he wrote an epic poem, <u>Africa,</u> on the Second Punic War.

Petrarch was also the first to refer to the period from the Fall of Rome to his own time as "The Dark Ages". Further, his Cicero discoveries inspired many educated persons to search for additional ancient documents.

Boccaccio (1313-1375), author of the <u>Decameron,</u> was among his friends and followers. He could read Greek and translated all the works of the Roman playwright Terence as well as Homer's <u>Iliad</u> and <u>Odyssey</u>. He stirred interest in Greek by inviting a scholar from Greek-speaking Constantinople to his home town, Florence, to teach that language and give lectures on Homer.

Another book-collecting enthusiast, *Tommaso of Saranza,* 1397-1455, only found lesser documents, but still greatly influenced the Renaissance after he became Pope.

Poggio Bracciolini, 1380-1459, was definitely the most successful manuscript hunter of this era. He was Secretary to the Roman Curia for 50 years, and a scholar. Poggio was also a famous scribe who invented his own distinctive style of calligraphy. Most of his "finds" occurred between 1415-17, when he searched the Benedictine Monasteries of Fulda, Cluny, St Gall, Langres, and Reichenau.

His life story is well researched and told in the Pulitzer Prize winning book by Stephen Greenblatt, The Swerve (2011). What matters for us, though, is the following list of ancient manuscripts Poggio introduced or re-introduced to the Latin world:

1415	Cluny	2 of *Cicero's* Orations
1416	St Gall	*Quintilian,* Institutio Oratoria
1417	Fulda	*Lucretius,* De Rerum Natura
1417	Langres	8 more Orations
1415-7		*Manilius,* Astronomica
1415-7		*Vitruvius,* De Architectura
1427	translation	*Diodorus of Sicily,* Universal History
1427	translation	Xenophon, Cyropaedia

Reflection #2: Looking at these events sequentially, I notice that the mathematical and medicinal works were the first classical works to become available. Philosophy and the battle over Aristotle was phase two. Finally came the softer sciences of art and literature.

With Petrarch, Boccaccio and Poggio, we witness the conclusion of a major, successful effort by leading and respected scholars to recover what they could of classic literature, sculpture, history, meteorology, architecture, and rhetoric.

This nearly completes our tale of the "Twisty Trail" that the masterpieces of Classical Greece followed: how the Macedonians and Romans embraced and embellished them; how they were largely lost to the West after 300 CE; and how they were then rescued by Muslims and Early Renaissance Scholars.

The invention of the printing press in the 1450s insured that these treasures would now survive. Also, one of the minor, but enthusiastic, manuscript hunters, Tommaso of Saranza, became Pope Nicholas V in 1447. Still a lover of Classical works, in 1448, he proposed creating a Vatican Library and donated 350 codices (parchment), including his own purchased copy of <u>Universal History</u> by *Diodorus of Sicily*. It now possesses 75,000 codices and 1.1 million books.

Yet, simply preserving all this was only the first step. Like the Sorcerer's apprentice, others wanted to see what else they could translate: Latin translations from the Greek originals of Archimedes, Aristotle, and Euclid stirred a desire to look at Greek versions of the New Testament (NT). The next chapter pursues this story and describes how this spurs the Protestant Reformation.

Equally important, the Ancient Greeks and Romans never saw their writings as static, but as a foundation for future writers with better data and different ideas. They had broad shoulders, and they wanted us to climb on them. Thomas Aquinas started this process by building on Aristotle and Averroes.

In our next chapter, <u>Blossoming Begins</u>, let's look at both the impact of renewed interest in original Greek versions of rediscovered documents, and some key instances of how Renaissance artists and sculptors embraced and applied the ideas of the Ancients.

Iconic Event: Petrarch is the best icon for this era.

He was the first to recover an ancient Roman document; others saw his life as marking the end of the Dark Ages. He demonstrated his love for Roman culture both by writing letters to his favorite ancient scholars and composing an Epic poem about the Punic wars. He was an important inspiration to his followers from Boccaccio to Poggio to Nicholas V who also helped bring Classical culture back to Italy.

The Twisty Trail

Chapter 14: BLOSSOMING BEGINS, 1400-1550

Since reviewing our cultural past together, we have observed governmental styles as well as followed the turbulent and twisty trail of our artistic and scientific heritage.

Government Style: Viewed from the perspective of whether there is a role for a popular voice, the high point over these years certainly was the practices of Athens and its island-based naval allies. These democracies lasted for only 171 years and ended in 338 when Macedonia defeated Athens at the Battle of Chaeronea. Rome and Carthage also provided a voice for all freedmen, though, in Rome at least, one of dubious effectiveness compared to their Senate. They were both Republics. Carthage's died in 212; Rome's in 46 BCE when Caesar became Dictator. Not much had happened in terms of democratic practices since!

As best we can tell, most other leaders between 100 and 1200 CE governed by divine right with absolute and inheritable kingships. One variation is kingship granted by a council of landed advisors who might or might not support the king's heir. Early Islamic caliphs come to mind as do the Germanic and Frankish tribes of Western Europe.

In 1215, though, English nobles forced King John to sign a Magna Carta that placed limits on the rights of any King of England. While giving no voice for the broader populace, it did limit the King's authority to infringe the rights of, at the beginning, its influential landed aristocracy. By 1246, its Parliament met regularly. Later, in 1341, England established a House of Commons to represent its non-noble wealthy merchant class. A voice for the general population in that House would evolve slowly over the ensuing centuries.

As Bamber Gascoigne notes in <u>The Story of Democracy</u> many other European kingships, besides England, already followed a similar pattern. By 1246, when England's Parliament began meeting regularly, similar assemblies already existed in France in the 12th century. Portugal had a *Cortes* in 1211; Leon, Castile and Catalonia also had them before 1246.

Many European kingships had also taken the step of creating a Third Estate to represent their wealthy merchant class. As early as 1188, the kingdom of Leon, in Spain, added burgers to its *Cortes* of nobles and clerics. Portugal established its Third Estate for the same purpose in 1254.

Both Gascoigne and Hudson, though, also note the rise of "communes" or free towns in Northern Italy and the Netherlands in the 1300s. These towns were products of rapid growth and wealth due to trade. These cities negotiated charters to obtain self-rule in exchange for taxes. They were independent of the kings and the landed aristocracies that surrounded them. Calling themselves democracies or republics, actual control often rested with local bankers, merchants, or guild leaders.

We can sniffle, if we wish, at these meager measures toward democracy. True, there is no role for popular input. As Gascoigne notes, though, they stand out starkly compared to the previous 1000 years. More importantly, these are the early signs of a more limited government and a wider popular participation that suggest the possibility of a coming Springtime.

Arts and Culture:

Donatello, 1386-1466, and *Brunelleschi*, 1377-1446, were both raised in Florence. They each learned their craft as apprentices in the workshop of the famous goldsmith, *Ghiberti*. Separately, in 1401, they bid on a contract to create bronze doors for the *Baptistery of Saint John* in Florence, but lost to Ghiberti. Donatello was about 16; Brunelleschi, 24. They then travelled to Rome and stayed until at least 1404. While other visitors marveled over the ruins; Donatello and Brunelleschi excavated and measured all the buildings, columns and sculpture parts, including the Pantheon. Others thought the two were mere treasure seekers, but these measurements showed the pair that the Classic Romans and Greeks understood and applied the principles of perspective in order to achieve a more lifelike and flexible style in their art. Brunelleschi's notes show that he discovered single-point linear perspective. This was a key to making the more lifelike art of the Renaissance possible! One scholar calls this "a decisive moment" in Italian Art History.

Donatello displays his early understanding of classic sculpture in his Saint George in 1417 and in his other works, mostly in Florence. His Masterpiece is his David (1430), probably the first male nude in centuries. David is naked with a hat and boots!

Then, in 1418, Brunelleschi won the contract to build the *Dome* for the Florence Cathedral. The cathedral was intended as the first example of a new building in the classical style. As such, its original architectural design called for an even larger dome than the Pantheon. No one at the time had any idea how to do it. This Dome was even more complex than that of the Pantheon. It would consume Brunelleschi's entire life, and is a supreme Renaissance achievement.

As the project progressed, workers found the hoists inadequate for lifting bricks to such a height. Fortuitously, Poggio's recent discovered copy of Vitruvius's De Architectura was already available and helped Brunelleschi address the issue.

These two artists from Florence had a significant influence on those who followed. A major difference between Medieval and Renaissance artists is the lifelike and informal appearance that we also associate with Classical Greece. The architects, sculptors and painters that followed enthusiastically applied linear perspective to their work and some achieved the excellence of DaVinci and Michelangelo. DaVinci's famous drawing, Vitruvian Man, is drawn from a similar figure in *Vitruvius's* De

Architectura and illustrates the principles of perspective as understood by Classical Greeks and Romans.

Back to the Original Greek:

Once scholars found translations of the Greco-Roman texts of their cultural bequest, it was inevitable that some would crave to read and translate these from the Greek originals. We saw this already in the instances of Aristotle, Euclid, and Archimedes. The surprise was the huge impact that followed when some scholars decided to take a second look at the Latin Bible!

Erasmus, 1469-1536, was a premier scholar of his age, a humanist from the Netherlands. Caught up in a desire to read the New Testament in the original Greek, he, with Church approval, wrote a new Latin NT in 1516. His second edition, released in 1519, displaced Saint Jerome's Vulgate, issued a millennium earlier.

Martin Luther, 1443-1546, noticed this. He produced his own fresh version of the whole Bible from the Greek and Hebrew to German. This enabled German speakers, who made up a large portion of the early Protestant Reformation, to read their newly-printed Bible for themselves. Martin wrote a NT version in 1522, but the OT waited until 1534. This was not Church sanctioned and helped spur the Protestant Reformation.

In England, *William Tyndale*, 1494-1536, inspired by Erasmus' 3rd Edition, began working on a Greek to

English NT translation that he produced over Royal (and Church) opposition in 1526. After his martyrdom in 1536, *John Rogers,* 1505-1555, and *Miles Coverdale,* 1488-1569, played roles in finishing the OT portion of his Bible. Tyndale was burned at the stake in 1536, as was Rogers in 1555. By that time the Reformation was fully in flower!

Philosophy:

Sometimes the impact of document recovery takes longer. But, it is equally deep. A prime example is Poggio's 1417 discovery of Lucretius' De Rerum Natura (On the Nature of Things). From Steven Greenblatt, The Swerve, we know of Lucretius' influence on Cicero and Virgil, but also on modern thinkers searching for an philosophy that fitted the Enlightenment. This ancient poem was first printed in 1473, translated into French in 1650, and English in 1683. Scholars credit it with impacting the thinking of Darwin, Nietzsche, and Freud.

Copernicus, 1473-1543:

Ptolemy's Almagest was the "holy grail" of desired texts for Arabs and the "bible" for over 1200 years when it came to understanding time, calendars, and eclipses; the movements of the planets and stars; or whether or not the earth was the center of the universe. Arabs were so driven to acquire a Greek copy that legend says they required one as part of the peace terms in a war with the Byzantines.

Only Aristarchus of Samos, 18 centuries before Copernicus, had ever argued that the sun was the center of the universe, and that the earth was in constant circulation around the sun. Such was the enormity of the change that now started!

Copernicus grew up in a prosperous family in a German-speaking part of Poland. He was well-educated in mathematics, theology, and astronomy, spending his years from 1491-1503 in Universities in Krakow, Padua and Bologna. He studied the writings of Aristotle, Aristarchus of Samos, Pythagoras, and Ptolemy, and he learned Greek so, by 1503, he could read the originals.

He used the observatories in Krakow, but began noting that his readings were inconsistent with an earth-centered universe. He published nothing about this at the time, but scholars have found a 40 page draft of his rationale, as of 1514, for positing a sun-centered universe. His book was ready to be published in 1524, and his friends urged him to do so.

There are extant notes, though, showing he knew this would subject him to "a risk of scorn" so he waited until 1543, the year of his death, to publish <u>On the Revolutions of the Celestial Spheres.</u> There was little initial controversy, but astronomers were slow to accept it until after the Galileo controversy seventy years later.

Reflection: Once Poggio and others recovered the lost Classical texts, and once Brunelleschi and Donatello showed what could happen with a return to classical culture and linear perspective, the world of art and architecture changed, sometimes quickly.

Similarly, Poggio's 1417 discovery of Lucretius' De Rerum Natura (On the Nature of Things), along with those of Cicero, heavily influenced subsequent literature and philosophy.

The key question, for me, is why did these discoveries ignite a response during these Renaissance years? After all, Europeans knew about Arabic numbers since 1000 CE, and they did nothing. What was different? Why were they now ready to drink the water of new knowledge?

In answer, William Henry Hudson's The Story of the Renaissance points to a series of inventions that led to major changes in people's attitude toward the key feudal institutions: the aristocracy and the church.

1. **Gunpowder.** Much of the power of nobles (landed aristocrats) depended on their fortresses, their combat skills and armor. First introduced by the English against the Scots in 1327, and against the French at Crecy (1346), gunpowder was an equalizer when peasants confronted fortifications and skilled knights.
2. **Mariners Compass.** Developed in the 1300's, it enabled mariners to boldly sail further and further from shore. In 1519-22, Magellan's ship completed a journey around the earth. This demonstrated that the earth was a sphere not a horizontal wheel as Isidore of Seville taught for so many centuries. The church, in 1327, had even burned a man for heresy

for saying the earth was round, not a wheel. When Magellan's ships did not fall off the earth, the church lost much credibility among the educated. Also, people in the Southern hemisphere were hard to explain away. They neither fell off the bottom of the wheel nor resembled descendants of the three sons of Noah!
3. **Printing Press.** Before printing, only the wealthy could afford books. After, the price of production declined and those of middling means could read these works for themselves. This undermined the authority of both the church and the nobles.

To the above, we must add the **growing political strength and independence of the merchant class**. In kingdoms, they obtained their power by dominating the Third Estate of the national parliament. Or they gained 'free town' status in Italy in places like Florence, Pisa, Bologna, Siena, and Genoa. They did the same outside Italy in places like Barcelona, Lubeck, Bruges or Ghent. The prosperity of these places showed that nobles and clerics were unneeded for the good life.

So, it is against this technological backdrop that the discovery of these classical documents occurred. This timing might account for their powerful impact.

The combined effect of finding Vitruvius and studying Roman ruins enabled creation of the largest dome in Europe and the discovery of a linear perspective that changed paintings, sculptures and architecture. Second, these rediscovered documents spurred new translations of the Bible that, in turn, fomented both Protestantism and literacy as Christians sought to read the Bible for themselves. Third, Copernicus' new heliocentric universe was an enormous event. It signaled that even Ptolemy's Almagest needed re-evaluation if there was better data. Acceptance of such changes in thinking would continue to take a long while for Europeans. But, it would come...just as it did for Arabic numbers, the zero, decimals, and algebra.

Iconic Event: I think the *Burning at the Stake of John Rogers*, drawn from Fox's, Book of Martyrs, fairly represents the Age. While we thrill to the excitement of

new discoveries, and some ideas were accepted quickly, others are strongly resisted. Certainly this was true for Copernicus, Lucretius, Luther, Tyndale and John Rogers.

Chapter 15: A BIRD'S EYE VIEW:

Looking back over these 6000 years, I suspect the reader has noticed some points of interest to them. Certainly, I have also learned a great deal!

1. <u>Democracy is rare and fragile.</u> Over these 60 centuries, Greek Democracy was the one that afforded the strongest role to the lower ranks of its population. The Roman Republic was next, though the effective role of its populace was limited compared to Greece. While there are signs of budding democracy in the Thirteenth Century, it is a wonder that by 1919 most Europeans were self-governed.
2. <u>Seafaring nations were more likely to produce republics, democracies and middle class wealth.</u> Carthage, Greece, the Low Countries, and England come to mind. They produced a powerful merchant class that required representation. Athens, we recall, even shared power with lowly rowers, upon whom their livelihoods depended. Land-based powers, by contrast, gained their land by conquest and seemed only to need the support of their lieutenants. (Perhaps, more research is needed here).
3. <u>Culture and Civilizations are easily lost.</u> The Glories of Greece survived only 170 years. Largely, they did so due to either providence or a 'twisty trail' of pure lucky happenstance. Or both. Persia, Assyria, Egypt, and Carthage likely produced great literature and thought, but little survived.

4. <u>Perspective made all the difference in Ancient Art.</u> Just compare the Classic lifelike Greek 'Zeus' (460 BCE) with that of Persian King Darius (521 BCE) or later kings. Medieval Christian Art lost perspective, but regained it through the Renaissance.
5. <u>Language and writing are important.</u> During this era, man progressed in writing from the technology of the clay tablet to papyrus to parchment to paper to printing. Each step further enabled a wider literacy.
6. <u>Islam, originally committed to increased learning, conveyed both their own, Persian, Indian, and Greek mathematical and scientific expertise back to the West.</u> My 'take away' is that at one time, these civilizations willingly learned from one another. Maybe both would benefit if we re-establish such attitudes.
7. <u>Aristotle still is "the" philosopher.</u> In a way, the Christian/Medieval era was about following up on the Platonic thread of Greek culture and dispensing with the Aristotelian notion that the nature of the universe was knowable and therefore worth pursuing. It did not go well! Bringing Aristotle back meant the natural world is now worth studying, and that holds the most promise for our future.

More can surely be noted, but a story like this means different things to different people, and at different stages of their lives. What questions and observations, dear reader, come to your mind? Who would you like to know more about? My fondest hope for this book is that it inspires you to follow a "twisty trail" of your own.

From Homer to Copernicus

The Twisty Trail

LIST OF MAPS:

1. Mediterranean world; by Dan Madden
   license: Public Domain   p. 13

2. Ancient Egypt and Mesopotamia, 1450 BCE; by Author; license: Public Domain   p. 17

3. Persian Empire, 490 BCE; by DHUSMA; license: Public Domain.   p. 25

4. Western Mediterranean, Carthage;
   By unknown;
   license: Public Domain.   p. 31

5. Pelopennesian War; by Marsayus;
   license: Public Domain.   p. 42

6. Western Mediterranean, 218 BCE; by Megistius;
   license: Public Domain.   p. 58

7. Roman Empire, 117 CE; by Andrea Nacu;
   license: Public Domain   p. 76

8. Umayyad Conquest; by RomaineO;
   License: Public Domain.   p. 100

9. Renaissance Europe, 1400; by Lynn Nelson;

license: Public Domain. Modified by Kathleen Konicek-Moran. p. 113

LIST OF IMAGES:

1. Hand-held Clay Tablet; Gavin.Collins; License: Public Domain. p. 15

2. Ramses II in Victory; by Nordisk familjebok; License: Public Domain p. 22

3. Behistun Iran Relief, 521 BCE; By Hara1603; license: Public Domain. p. 27

4. Bust of Homer; britishmuseum.com; by JW108; license: Public Domain. p. 32

5. Greek Theater; by publicdomainpictures.net; license: Public Domain. p. 34

6. Atarxerxes; by Walter Crane; license: Public Domain. p. 39

7. Zeus at Olympia; by Phidias, Quatremere de Quincy; license: US Public Domain p. 47

8. Dionysius Sarcophagus; by NY Metropolitan Museum; license: Public Domain. p. 56

9. Triumph with Bearers of trophies; by Andrei Mantegna;
   license: wikipedia, US Public Domain   p. 62

10. Bust of Sulla; by unknown, Munich Glyptothek;
    licensed: Public Domain   p. 72

11. Crossing the Rubicon; by Jacob Abbot;
    license: Public Domain.   p. 77

12. Internal Pantheon Light; by RichjHeath;
    license: Public Domain.   p. 85

13. Saint Jerome in his Study, by Drurer;
    US Public Domain.   p. 98

14. House of Wisdom; by ar.wkipedia.org;
    license: US Public Domain.   p. 107

15. Francesco Petrarcha; by von Gustav Schauer;
    license: commons.wikimedia.org, US Public Domain   p. 118

16. Donatello's David; by RenArt88;
    license: Public Domain   p. 124

17. Santa Maria de Fiore; by Enna;
    license: Public Domain.   p. 125

18. "burning of John Rogers"; by Unknown;
    license: Public Domain.   p. 131

Back Cover: Copernicus; US public domain.

The Twisty Trail

SELECT BIBLIOGRAPHY:

Books:

Beard, Mary, SPQR, Kindle, 2015.

Duncan, Michael, Storm before the Storm, Kindle, 2017.

Ehrman, Bart, The Triumph of Christianity, Kindle, 2018.

Everitt, Anthony, The Rise of Athens, 2016.

Freeman, Charles, Egypt, Greece and Rome, 2004.

Greenblatt, Stephen, The Swerve, 2011.

Harrison, Richard, Spain at the Dawn of History, 1988.

Hudson, William Henry, The Story of the Renaissance, Kindle, 1996.

King, Ross, Brunelleschi's Dome, 2000.

Lewis, David Levering, God's Crucible, 2008.

Lyons, Jonathan, The House of Wisdom, Kindle, 2009.

Pettegree, Andrew, Brand Luther, Kindle, 2015.

Roberts, Jennifer, The Plague of War, Kindle, 2017.

Starr, Chester, A History of the Ancient World, 1991.

Waters, Matt, Ancient Persia, Kindle, 2014.

Lecture Series:

Freedman, Paul, Online Lecture Series, Early Middle Ages, Yale University, 2012. Chapters of particular interest are: "Constantine and the Early Church"; " St Augustine's Confessions", "Monasticism", and "Splendor of the Abbasids".

Instructables.com has a site with a Video that shows "How to Make a Clay Tablet".

Internet:

I used both Brittanica.com and Wikepedia.com to supplement and confirm information. I liked the way they organized the information. Attributions for specific articles are in the Endnotes for the appropriate chapter.

Other sites I found especially helpful were:

Andrews, Evan, History.com, "8 Legendary Ancient Libraries".

Gascoigne, Bamber, "Story of Democracy", Historyworld.net, from 2001 ongoing.

Eduscapes.com website "Ancient Libraries; 300s and 800s CE".

newworldencyclopedia.org, articles on the House of Wisdom, Al Kindi, and Al Khwarizmi..

The Twisty Trail

ENDNOTES:

Chapter 1:

Sources: My key sources for the Bronze Age are Charles Freeman, Egypt, Greece and Rome, 2004, (pp. 19-33), and Chester Starr, A History of the Ancient World, 1991 (pp.27-98). I encourage the reader also to google Brittanica.com for additional information and images of papyrus, cuneiform script, clay tablets, and royal inscriptions to get a clearer sense of the nature of the primary sources available from this period. Also, Instructables.com has a site that shows "How to Make a Clay Tablet" which clarifies the process. In addition, Wikipedia.com has lists of "Ancient Literature" and "Ancient Egyptian Papyrus" that provide a flavor of what has survived!

Chapter 2:

Sources: Both Freeman (pp. 94-120) and Starr (pp. 99-142), cited earlier, continue as important background for this essay, but Matt Water's Ancient Persia, 2014, is my key source for the rise of Persia, the early Achaemenid dynasty, and the type of records available (pp. 19-33; 34-99; 8-18). He has an eye for detail and a pro-Persian perspective that I found refreshing.

Chapter 3:

Sources: Greece excepted, we know even less about the Western Mediterranean than we do about the early Persians. For Greece, I have relied on both Freeman, (pp. 185-274) and Starr, (pp. 185-224), cited earlier. For others, I used (pp. 53-130), for early Rome: and, for Athens, Anthony Everitt, The Rise of Athens, 2016, (pp. 79-104).

Chapter 4:

Sources: Matt Waters, Ancient Persia, (pp. 120-260); Mary Beard, SPQR, (pp. 91, 98, 131-169); Jennifer Roberts, The Plague of War, 2017, (pp. 19-32); and Anthony Everitt, The Rise of Athens, (pp. 114-140).

Chapter 5:

Sources: in addition to Freeman (pp. 198-214; 271--313) and Starr (pp. 319-358), Jennifer Roberts, The Plague of War, (pp., 333-362), was particularly helpful. She intertwines the events of the Peloponnesian War with the Theater of the times! I also found internet sites such as Brittanica.com and Wikepedia.com very valuable on specific individuals including Phidias, Kritios, Praxiteles, Aeschylus, Euripides, and Aristophanes and Aristotle.

Chapter 6:

Sources: Both Freeman (pp. 314-332; 333-353) and Starr (pp. 393-436) provide excellent accounts of both

Alexander's Campaigns and Hellenistic cultural progress. Alexander brought 13 historians along on his campaigns. Though none of their works survive, other writers cite several of them. I also found internet sites such as Brittanica.com and Wikepedia.com very valuable for details on the cultural achievements of specific individuals. Also, the eduscapes.com website "Ancient Libraries; 200s BCE" and history.com's "8 Legendary Ancient Libraries", (Evan Andrews), were fascinating!

Chapter 7:

Sources: Both Freeman (pp. 383-401) and Starr (pp. 477-501) provide excellent background on this period of Greco-Roman interaction, including cultural. I also relied much on Mary Beard's SPQR, (pp. 131-169). The internet sites, Brittanica.com and Wikepedia.com, are valuable for additional details on the cultural achievements of specific individuals including Polybius, Terence, Pictor, and Cato the Elder.

Chapter 8:

Sources: The accounts of Mary Beard's SPQR (pp. 209-252) and especially Mike Duncan The Storm Before the Storm (2017) shaped my way of looking at the period. I also found internet sites such as Brittanica.com and Wikepedia.com very valuable for details on the Cimbri Wars, Marius, Pompey, Mithridates, and Sulla.

Chapter 9:

Sources: This is a controversial era. Both Freeman (pp. 450-464) and Starr (pp. 525-546) provide important background to any understanding of the basic facts. Both Mary Beard's SPQR (pp. 253-296) and Robert Harris' novel, Dictator, influenced my perspective. Further, I particularly admired the informative summaries on the internet sites, Brittanica.com and Wikepedia.com, for details on Julius Caesar, Augustus, and Pompey and the Pantheon.

Chapter 10:

Sources: Freeman (pp. 564-627) and Starr (pp. 603-625) and Beard (pp. 337-386) each provide fine chapters on the cultural and scientific advances of this Golden Age. For supplementary information, I again found the internet sites, Brittanica.com and Wikepedia.com helpful for details on the cultural achievements of specific individuals such as *Diodorus of Sicily* and *Cicero* as well as the construction of the Pantheon. Other helpful sites were History.com on Julius Caesar and ancient.eu on Roman Medicine

Chapter 11

Sources: For Early Christianity, Constantine and Constantinople, there are several key sources. In addition to Freeman, Egypt, Greece and Rome , 2004, (pp. 564-604), I recommend Paul Freedman's Lecture series, Early Middle Ages, Yale, 2012, including "Constantine and the Early Church", " St Augustine's Confessions" and "Monasticism". Additionally, Bart Ehrman's The Triumph of Christianity provides insight into the key differences between paganism and the monotheistic faiths; he also has an excellent treatment of scholarly thought on measuring the actual size of Christian population over the centuries. As usual, I also found internet sites Brittanica.com and of that time Wikepedia.com had valuable details on specific individuals, such as Boethius, Isidore of Seville, Augustine, Jerome, and Benedict of Nursia. Also, the eduscapes.com website "Ancient Libraries; 300s CE" and history.com's "8 Legendary Ancient Libraries", (Evan Andrews) give perspective on the Libraries at Constantinople and Rome at the time!

Chapter 12

Sources: Besides Paul Freeman's lecture "Splendor of the Abbasids" in the Yale Series, cited above, I drew heavily from Jonathan Lyons, The House of Wisdom, 2009, for the Abbasids (especially ch.3) and for the Spanish Umayyads. David Levering Lewis', God's Crucible, 2008, (mostly chapters 8,10, and 12) emphasize cultural events in Islamic Spain. Further, Brittanica.com and Wikepedia.com helped confirm details about Al-Khwarizmi and newworldencyclopedia.org did the same for Al Kindi. The House of Wisdom is cited in the eduscapes.com website "Ancient Libraries; 800 CE" and history.com's "8 Legendary Ancient Libraries", (Evan Andrews).

Chapter 13

Sources: Both Jonathan Lyons, The House of Wisdom, and David Levering Lewis', God's Crucible have important chapters on the diffusion of Arabic knowledge to Western Europe. Paul Freeman's lecture "Splendor of the Abbasids" in the Yale Series, cited above, introduced me to the conflict over Aristotle at the University of Paris. Also, Stephen Greenblatt's, The Swerve, 2011, tells Poggio's story in detail. Additional information on Aquinas, Moerbeke, Abelard, Petrarch, Poggio and Nickolas V came from Brittanica.com and Wikepedia.com.

Chapter 14

Sources: The discussion on the growth of democracy comes from Bamber Gascoigne, Story of Democracy, HistoryWorld.com, 2001, p. 2. Ross King's, Brunelleschi's Dome, 2000, provides wonderful detail on this amazing achievement of the Early Renaissance. Andrew Pettegree's, Brand Luther, 2015, taught me the importance of the nascent German printing industry and Luther's new German Bible to the success of the Reformation movement. William Henry Hudson, Story of the Renaissance, 1996, is both a good general history and a source of colorful detail. Other information on Donatello, Erasmus, Tyndale, John Rogers, Coverdale, and Copernicus came from Brittanica.com and Wikepedia.com.

From Homer to Copernicus

The Twisty Trail

APPENDIX:

1. **Rise of the Persian Empire.**
2. **Campaigns of Alexander**
3. **Hellenistic Libraries**
4. **Cimbri Wars**
5. **Some Ancient Historians**

Rise of the Persian Empire:

Two generations after the Battle of Carchemish, Persia, one of Babylon's allies in the battle, began building an empire of its own. **Cyrus the Great** started by defeating the Medes, who occupied the lands just north of Babylon and Assyria, in 550 BCE. Then, with help from the Medes he just defeated, he conquered Lydia in far western Anatolia. The next year, 539, his growing coalition decisively defeated Babylon.

After **Cyrus** died In 530, his son Cambyses became king, and continued their legacy by successfully invading Egypt from 525-522. Next was **Darius the Great.** A famed "Bisitun Inscription and Relief" on a mountainside, dated 520/19 BCE, proclaims Darius's rulership from the Indus River to Libya and from the Danube to the Sudan: his entire known civilized world. In 510, Darius founded a new Persian capital, Persepolis; he also successfully invaded Eastern Europe (Thrace, Bulgaria and some western Anatolian ports along the Aegean Sea).

Some of the cities and islands in Western Anatolia revolted in 499 BCE. Darius, focused on Egypt and attacks from the northeast, charged Mardonius, his son in law, with suppressing these uprisings on the periphery of the Empire. He did so successfully, and ruthlessly! To punctuate his determination, Darius authorized an expedition in 490 BCE to punish Athens, a city that had helped fund the rebels.

Persian Wars with Greece. As of 480 BCE, Persians had always been victorious in its major battles! Likely, their kings viewed the Greek victory at Marathon (490) as a temporary set-back for the undersized (40,000 men) punitive expedition Darius sent to avenge Greek destruction of Sardis, Persia's westernmost provincial capital. Both sides knew the Persians were coming back!

The defeat of Xerxes huge 480 BCE expedition of 600 ships and perhaps 150,000 men (Herodotus claimed 1,500,000, but few scholars accept that) could not be so easily ignored. Yes, Xerxes had defeated the Spartans at Thermopylae and sacked Athens, but Persia's naval allies loss at Salamis of 200+ ships, combined with 200 more ships lost to storms, forced Xerxes to withdraw both the remaining ships that supplied his troops as well as most of his infantry. Worse, the 40,000 men that Xerxes left behind lost decisively to an alliance of Athenian, Spartan and Platean troops.

Salamis marked the end of Persian expansion into Greece, and it began an era of Athenian hegemony in the Aegean Sea. From 479-467, the Athenian Admiral Cimon constantly attacked and defeated Persian naval forces. In 449 BCE, Persia formally recognized de-facto Athenian control in the Aegean.

The Campaigns of Alexander:

After Granicus, Alexander sent his army down the Aegean coast of Anatolia (Turkey) where there were many Greek port cities and "liberated" them. This also secured his rear against a Persian landing of military transports.

Darius lll, who had just become king in 335 BCE, then met, and lost to, Alexander in a closely contested battle in September of 333 at Issus, near Babylon. Once again, Alexander shrewdly moved his armies south to secure his rear by capturing all the seaports of Phoenicia. He also "liberated" Egypt where citizens greeted him as a god. After founding the Greek colony city of Alexandria, he turned north to confront Darius again.

In the single year of 331 BCE, Alexander defeated Darius at Gaugamela, sacked the Royal Palace at Persepolis in Persia, and, after Darius was killed by his own supporters, declared himself king of the Persian Empire. Since this included parts of India, he spent the next nine years in Bactria and India trying to bring them back into his new Empire. Wounded in India, he died in Babylon in 323.

Hellenistic Libraries:

The Ptolemies funded **The Great Library of Alexandria** (est. 306 BCE) and committed it to collect a copy of every extant book. This included the Hebrew Septuagint which was translated into Greek sometime between 283-246 BCE. Ultimately, the Library obtained 400,000 to 700,000 scrolls, mostly papyrus. Their specialties included medicine, science, Homer, and commentaries on Homer.

The Seleucids supported **The Royal Library of Antioch,** established about 221 BCE. Antioch, in modern Syria, was the capital of their Empire, and, by 68 BCE, the second largest city in the Mediterranean.

Athens City Archives had complete collections of Homer, Hesiod, and most of the great tragedies. Further, private collections there included the invaluable libraries of Plato's **Academy** and Aristotle's **Lyceum.**

Pergamum was a very Greek city in central Anatolia. Its king built this library just after 197 BCE. It was second in size and prestige only to Alexandria. At its peak, it included about 200,000 scrolls. Most were of parchment, made from sheep leather, rather than papyrus (because the Alexandrians cut off their papyrus supplies), and as it happened, lasted longer .

The impact of these libraries was enormous: they preserved the Classic writings for generations, and helped spread knowledge about them throughout the whole Eastern Mediterranean. Greek became the language of educated persons throughout the East.

The Cimbri Wars:

As of 105 BCE, Rome only controlled the southern two thirds of the Italian peninsula! Before that, Romans relied on Celtic allies to assist them in the Alpine regions. In both 113 and 109, these allies had asked Rome to help against the Cimbri, a huge tribe with 150,000 warriors. In both instances, when Rome marched north to assist their allies, Cimbri completely overwhelmed Rome and its allies, but the Cimbri decided to move west rather than south into a vulnerable Italy.

Then, in 105 BCE, the Cimbri came again asking for land to settle in. This time, the Senate dispatched **two** armies with a total of 80,000 men and two consuls. In the Battle of Arausio, along the Rhone River, both Roman units, their 40,000 camp followers, and their allies were all slaughtered. Rome was in a total panic as all its remaining legions were tied up in Africa and an insurrection in Sicily. Luckily, the Cimbri once again decided to go West.

This gave the Roman Senate some time to prepare. They appointed Gaius Marius, a recent victor over the Numidians, as consul to lead the Roman armies on the Gallic frontier. They did so, even though he was ineligible, having already been a consul the year before. They did so, even though he was a *populare*, the political group committed to weakening Senatorial power. They did so, even though Marius, due to a lack of available Roman small landowners, needed and received a special exemption to recruit soldiers from the poorer classes (because up to then only landed-persons could serve in the army).

When the Cimbri and their allies returned in 102 BCE, Marius was ready. His training regimen had emphasized fitness and mobility to the point that the new legions could carry their own supplies and not need to wait for a baggage train. He, also, supplied them with new javelins whose tips broke off after landing so the enemy could not throw them back at the Romans. With six legions (40,000 men), Marius first confronted 120,000 Teutones and Ambrones near Aquae Sextiae (along the Rhone) and killed or captured 100,000 of them. Then, at Vercellae near the River Po, Marius and his cavalry leader, Lucius Sulla, combined their 50,000 men to defeat the Cimbri so decisively that they captured 60,000 and killed 120,000.

This ended the Cimbri threat!

Ancient Historians:

Early Greece produced three historians whose writings provide our primary windows to what happened in the entire Mediterranean region.

Herodotus's Histories *(440 BCE)* describe the background and culture of the major provinces that made up the Persian Empire plus the tale of the Persian War with Greece. It is the sole narrative we have for this period and for the nations involved.

Thucydides personally participated in the Peloponnesian War that he describes in his The Peloponnesian Wars (395 BCE).

Xenophon wrote both the Hellenica (also about Peloponnesian War) and Anabasis, (a campaign he participated in as a mercenary against the Persian King, Artaxerxes), both between 405-395.

Among Romans, there were four of particular note:

Diodorus of Sicily (90 to 30 BCE): a Greek historian who wrote a Universal History of 40 books (only 5 survive) covering the time from ancient Greece to Julius Caesar.

Sallust (86 to 35 BCE): a Roman *populare* who wrote about both the Cataline Conspiracy (68 BCE) and the corruption surrounding The Jugurthine War (105-100 BCE).

Livy (59 to 17 BCE): a Roman historian whose <u>Ab Urbe Condita Libri</u> covers the period from the founding of the Roman Republic to Augustus. He successfully urged Emperor Claudius to study and write history.

Dionysius of Halicarnassus (60 BCE to 7 BCE): a Greek historian who wrote in Latin, taught rhetoric, and sought to reconcile Greek speakers to Roman rule. His master achievement is <u>Roman Antiquities,</u> a primary source for the early legends about the founding of Rome, including Romulus, Remus, and the early wars with the Sabines.

INDEX:

Abbasids 101, 102, 104, 105, 144, 151, 152
Abelard 110, 152
Achaemenids 36
Aeschylus 32, 43, 148
Al Khwarizmi 102, 112, 145
Al Kindi 104, 105, 112, 145, 151
Alexander 48, 49, 51, 52, 54, 55, 60, 85, 149, 155, 157
Alexandria 51, 52, 53, 55, 83, 84, 92, 157, 158
Almagest 84, 104, 106, 112, 127, 131
Antioch 52, 53, 59, 89, 109, 110, 111, 158
Aphrodite of Cnidius 45
Aquinas 112, 114, 115, 118, 152
Archimedes 54, 112, 115, 117, 126
Aristarchus 54, 84, 127, 128
Aristophanes 32, 43, 44, 148
Aristotle 37, 44, 46, 48, 79, 82, 95, 104, 106, 112, 113, 114, 117, 118, 126, 128, 134, 148, 152, 158
Artaxerxes 39, 161
Athena Parthenos 45
Athens 30, 32, 34, 35, 36, 37, 41, 43, 45, 49, 53, 54, 59, 69, 121, 133, 143, 148, 156, 158
Augustine 95, 144, 151
Augustus 76, 77, 81, 82, 85, 86, 87, 150, 162
Avicenna 112
Barry Powell
  Powell 33
Battle of Carchemish 24, 155
Behistun 25, 26, 35, 36, 139
Behistun, 25
Benedict 96, 151
Boccaccio 115, 117, 119
Boethius 95, 104, 110, 151
Bronze Age 14, 16, 21, 147
Brunelleschi 123, 124, 125, 128, 143, 152
Byblos 20, 24
Caesar 70, 73, 74, 75, 77, 78, 79, 80, 84, 87, 89, 121, 150, 161

Campanus 110
Carthage 29, 30, 37, 38, 57, 58, 59, 62, 65, 81, 121, 133, 134
Cato the Elder 38, 60, 62, 149
Chaeronea 49, 121
Cicero 30, 65, 75, 79, 80, 82, 115, 116, 127, 129, 150
Cimbri 66, 71, 150, 155, 159, 160
Commentaries on the Gallic Wars 80
Constantine 87, 90, 91, 92, 93, 144, 151
Copernicus 87, 127, 128, 131, 132, 141, 153
Cordoba 104, 105, 106, 112
Corinth 35, 49, 60, 61, 89
Crassus 73, 74, 79
Crete 20
Cyrus the Great 36, 52, 155
Darius the Great 25, 155
De Architectura 77, 83, 86, 116, 125, 126
Democritus 45, 54, 82
Diocletian 87, 89
Dionysian Artists 53
Dionysian Festival 34
Dionysus Festival 43
Dioscordes 88
Dioscorides 103, 104, 106
Dome for the Florence Cathedral 124
Donatello 123, 124, 128, 140, 152
Egypt 12, 14, 15, 18, 19, 20, 21, 22, 23, 24, 27, 35, 51, 52, 59, 75, 91, 100, 104, 133, 137, 143, 147, 151, 155, 156, 157
Elements 54, 102, 106, 110
Epic of Gilgamesh. 26
Epicurus 54, 82
Erasmus 126, 152
Euclid 54, 102, 104, 105, 110, 112, 117, 126
Euripides 32, 43, 44, 148
Fibonacci 111
Flamininus 59
Gaius Gracchus 66
Galen 83, 88, 103, 104, 112
Gerard 111
Gerbert 106, 107
Gilgamesh Epic 19
Great Harris Papyrus 16
Great Library of Ashurbanipal 25, 26
Great Library of Constantinople 90, 92
Great Pyramid of Giza 16

Great Royal Road 23
Greece 5, 11, 12, 21, 29, 30, 31, 33, 34, 35, 37, 38, 41, 44, 47, 48, 49, 51, 55, 59, 60, 65, 68, 101, 117, 125, 133, 143, 147, 148, 151, 156, 157, 161
Herodotus 33, 43, 156, 161
Hesiod 31, 158
Hippocrates 45
Hittite clay tablets 15
Hittites 19, 20, 21, 22, 23
Hittites, 19, 20, 21, 23
Homer 11, 30, 32, 33, 34, 77, 115, 139, 158
HOMER 1, 32
Horace 81, 86
House of Wisdom 101, 102, 103, 104, 105, 107, 140, 143, 145, 151, 152
Isidore of Seville 96, 129, 151
Isocrates 40, 44, 49
Israelites 23, 36
Jerome 91, 97, 126, 140, 151
Jesus 89, 90
Judea 23, 97
Kadesh 19, 22
King Artaxerxes 35
King Ashurbanipal 15, 24
King Ashurbanipal's Library 15
King's Peace 39
Knossos 20
Kritios Boy 44
Lamentation on the Destruction of Ur 19
Linear b 21
Lucretius 54, 82, 116, 127, 129, 132
Lysippus 54
Macedonia 48, 51, 55, 59, 60, 65, 75, 85, 121
Magna Carta 121
Marius 67, 68, 69, 70, 73, 74, 150, 159, 160
Martin Luther 126
Menander 53, 60
Mithridates 68, 69, 70, 73, 74, 75, 150
Mohammed 99
Mount Pangaeus 48
Octavian 75, 76, 77
of *Constantine* 90
oligarchy 41
On the Measurement of the Circle 54, 112, 115
On the Nature of Things 54, 82, 127, 129
On the Revolutions of the Celestial Spheres. 128
optimares 65, 69, 71, 73
ostracize 42

Ovid 81, 86
Pantheon 77, 82, 86, 88, 123, 124, 140, 150
Parthenon 45
Paul 90, 92, 95, 144, 151, 152
Peloponnesian Wars 36, 41, 161
Pergamum 51, 53, 69, 83, 103, 158
Persia 18, 23, 25, 27, 33, 35, 36, 37, 39, 40, 43, 49, 51, 52, 55, 75, 100, 101, 104, 106, 133, 144, 147, 148, 155, 156, 157
Persian King Darius 14
Petrarch 115, 117, 118, 152
Phidias 45, 47, 139, 148
Philip 48, 49, 51, 52
Philip II 48
Philippics 49
Phoenicia 20, 22, 23, 157
Pictor 38, 60, 149
Pisistratus 32, 34
Plato 46, 79, 82, 90, 95, 104, 158
Plautus 53, 60
Poggio 116, 117, 119, 125, 127, 128, 129, 152
Polybius 53, 60, 117, 149
Pompey 68, 70, 73, 74, 75, 79, 150
populare 67, 70, 73, 160, 161
Praxilites 45
Ptolemy 51, 84, 88, 104, 106, 112, 127, 128, 131
quatrimenes 58
Quintilian 80, 116
Ramses III. 17
Rogers 127, 131, 132, 140, 152
Rome 5, 29, 30, 37, 38, 52, 53, 57, 59, 60, 61, 63, 65, 67, 68, 69, 70, 74, 75, 76, 78, 81, 82, 83, 84, 85, 88, 89, 90, 91, 92, 99, 115, 121, 123, 143, 147, 148, 151, 159, 162
Rosetta Stone 14
Sicily 29, 37, 57, 58, 59, 65, 66, 75, 110, 116, 150, 159, 161
Siger of Brant 114
Solon 31
Sophocles 32, 43
Sosigenes, 84
Sparta 31, 35, 40, 41
Sulla 68, 69, 70, 71, 73, 74, 140, 150, 160
Syracuse 44, 57, 61, 62, 110
Terence 60, 115, 149
Thales of Miletus 31

The Book of the Dead   16
The Dark Ages   115
The Eloquent Peasant,   17
the Royal Road   18
Thebes   24, 35, 48, 49, 51
Theodosius   87, 90, 94
Theogony   31, 33
thetes   34, 42
Thucydides   33, 43, 161
Thutmose I   16
Toledo   109, 111, 112
Tommaso of Saranza 116, 117
Trajan   82, 88
Tyndale 126, 127, 132, 152
Tyre   20, 29, 30
Umayyad   100, 105, 137
Universal History 53, 117, 161
University of Paris 113, 152
Vatican Library   117
Virgil 77, 81, 86, 115, 127
Vitruvius 77, 83, 86, 116, 125, 130
Vulgate   97, 126
Wheel of Fortune 5, 67, 71, 85, 95, 104, 109
William of Moerbeke   115
Works and Days   31, 33
Xenophon 33, 43, 116, 161
Zaragoza   105
Zeus at the Temple in Olympia   45
ziggurats   18

Made in the USA
Lexington, KY
22 November 2019